120 MINUTES TO
LIVE
BIG

Do Away With Small Living

DEREK GRIER

120 Minutes to Live Big: Do Away With Small Living

by Derek Grier

copyright ©2018

ISBN: 978-1-943294-83-1

cover design by Martijn van Tilborgh

CONTENTS

SECTION 13: PERSONAL GROWTH

SECTION 14: RELATIONSHIPS

ACKNOWLEDGMENTS

My deepest love and admiration to my wife, Yeromitou. Your strength and kindness inspire me. You are a gift from God.

Derek and David, thank you for sharing your dad with the demands of ministry.

Mom and Dad, thanks for your support and encouragement.

Shani McKenzie and the Grace Church Working Group, I appreciate your input.

Acknowledgments are also due two people who are now in the presence of God, but who have no less contributed to this book.

To the late Karen Prewitt, my administrative assistant, thanks for your faithfulness in doing a very tedious and challenging job.

To the late Dr. Myles Munroe, you saw something in me, before I saw it in myself.

INTRODUCTION

It is *the moments that make the minute* and the minutes that make the hour, the strokes of the brush that make the painting and the notes that make the song. It seems all big things come from how we handle the small.

In 2007, my congregation moved from a high school across town and purchased a building in a different and economically challenged neighborhood. Our attendance dropped from a couple hundred to less than thirty. We had a new $1.2 million mortgage and were facing considerable cash overruns and terribly low morale.

I prayed for a miracle, but I had a sneaking suspicion that a quick fix was not in order. Strangely, a statement by one of my college math professors kept coming to mind: "Students, the answer is always in the problem; you just have to learn to extract it." I knew the answer was somehow in our problem, but I needed the wisdom of God to find it.

I set aside some time to pray, and I felt very strongly that I should go on the radio. The idea was at first irritating because there was no way we could have afforded a thirty-minute program. It made no sense to even imagine such a thing, but the idea lingered. I clearly could not afford a radio program. If this idea was an answer to prayer, I had to shift my thinking. Instead of focusing on what I could not afford, I had to begin to focus on what I could afford. I could not pay for a thirty-minute program, but I could find a way to fund a few sixty-second radio spots.

My wife and I went out on a limb, trusting my time in prayer. We activated our line of credit attached to our home, and the *Ministry Minute* was born. If I was wrong, we would lose our home, and I would lose our church, whatever was left of my confidence, and probably my self-respect. I have heard others say that faith is spelled r-i-s-k. We were taking one of the biggest financial risks of our lives.

I had only sixty seconds to give a meaningful and memorable message that would radically impact the life of the listener. I prayed, studied, and worked hours each day to fit hour-long messages into the one-minute format. The *Minutes* aired, and they became an area phenomenon. By the end of the first year over one thousand people had visited our church. By the end of 2011, we were holding four services every Sunday to keep up with the demand. Many Sundays people turned away because we were out of seating. Today we are in a new facility, have thousands of members, and reach millions weekly on our radio programs, television programs, and websites—but none of this would have happened if we did not first learn the value of the minute.

Sometimes we do not move forward in life because we do not believe we have been given enough to work with. This is tragic. God never holds us responsible for what we do not have but for whether we use what we do have. This book includes the first years of radio minutes that aired on 104.1 FM in DC. This book comes out of a life of a lot of hard learning and tough living. Join with me on a journey to make every minute of your life matter.

section 1
HAPPINESS

⏰ minute 1

CHOOSE TO BE HAPPY

Abraham Lincoln experienced long bouts of depression. He eventually made this statement: "Most people are as happy as they make up their mind to be."[1] If you live long enough, you will discover true happiness does not come from events alone but from a choice. You have to choose to be happy. The word *happy* derives partly from the word *happenstance*, indicating that a person's happiness is at the mercy of the stuff that "happens" to us externally. But true joy is internal and comes from a source within. James 1:2 says, "Consider it pure joy, my brothers, whenever you face trials of many kinds." What does *consider* mean?

It means, simply, to think through something until you can make a decision. In other words, when we face trials, it is up to us to decide our response. James states further, "Perseverance must finish its work so that you can be mature and complete, not lacking anything" (James 1:4). He promises that only those of us who choose joy end up mature and complete. We may not be able to control what happens to us, but we can certainly control our response. There are times when we need to cry, but at some point, we must dry our eyes and make the choice to go ahead with living.

 **takeaway**

What negative life circumstances have you "considered" pure joy and how did it affect your spiritual maturity?

reflect

_____

_____

_____

_____

_____

_____

_____

_____

_____

_____

_____

_____

_____

minute 2

FINDING OUR MEASURE

After a major milestone, I asked myself whether I was finally successful. But as I searched my heart, I was stumped because I had never really defined success. I searched for a definition but drew a blank. Then I thought about Jesus. He never went to college. He never wrote a book and certainly was not a multimillionaire. Jesus' impact on humanity has been determined not by all He amassed in His life but by all He left behind.

JESUS' IMPACT ON HUMANITY HAS BEEN DETERMINED NOT BY ALL HE AMASSED IN HIS LIFE BUT BY ALL HE LEFT BEHIND.

In Luke 22:28–29, He says, "You are those who have stood by me in my trials. And I confer on you a kingdom, just as my father conferred one on me." In other words, Jesus lived to leave a legacy. The ultimate yardstick of success is not measured by how much we have taken for ourselves in this life but by how much we have left behind for others when we go to the next.

 **takeaway**

How would you define success?
Does it align with Jesus' definition
of success?

reflect

_____

_____

_____

_____

_____

_____

_____

_____

_____

_____

_____

⏱ minute 3

LAUGHTER

Zora Neale Hurston once commented, "I love myself when I am laughing."[2] As a person who wears a lot of hats—husband, father, brother, pastor, and friend—there is something about laughter that lightens my load and helps bring things back into perspective. Psalm 2:4 states, "The One enthroned in heaven laughs." It goes on to explain He laughs because of His enemies. Why does God laugh? Because He knows that in the end, His team always wins.

REAL FAITH LEARNS TO LAUGH AT TEMPORARY SETBACKS, EVEN AT MOMENTARY SHORTCOMINGS, BECAUSE WE KNOW IN THE END WE ARE ON THE WINNING TEAM.

Real faith puts an expiration date on our moments of sorrow. Real faith learns to laugh at temporary setbacks, even at momentary shortcomings, because we know in the end we are on the winning team. Let's not take ourselves so seriously! It may seem like your problem is going to get the last word, but the battle is the Lord's, and He is going to have the last laugh.

 **takeaway**

What setbacks and crises have you faced and how has humor helped you overcome them?

reflect

_____

_____

_____

_____

_____

_____

_____

_____

_____

_____

_____

_____

section 2
MARRIAGE & FAMILY RELATIONSHIPS

⏰ minute 4

SHOW PEOPLE YOU CARE

John Maxwell, leadership expert, states, "People do not care how much you know until they know how much you care."[3] In other words, before you attempt to direct, you must connect. One day, my younger brother and I had a heated disagreement over the phone. After I got off the phone, my conscience was bothering me, and I defended myself, thinking, *I know I was right.* Instantly, the Holy Spirit spoke to me. "You were right. But were you kind?"

SOMETIMES WINNING THE ARGUMENT IS NOT AS IMPORTANT AS MAINTAINING A RELATIONSHIP.

Sometimes winning the argument is not as important as maintaining a relationship. Proverbs 15:28 says, "The heart of the righteous weighs its answers." Think before you speak.

 **takeaway**

Are there relationships that have been damaged by your impulsive speech? What will it take to restore them?

reflect

_____

_____

_____

_____

_____

_____

_____

_____

_____

_____

THE "IGNORANT TOOL"

The other day, a friend and I put together a basketball hoop for my boys. About two hours into the ninety-degree evening, we reached for the hammer to make a part fit. It reminded me of when I was a kid. My father and I would try to fix something, and if we did not have the tools to fix it, Dad would say, "Son, hand me the ignorant tool." He would grab the hammer and beat the thing into submission.

IT TAKES SKILL AND GRACE TO COMMUNICATE, BUT IT DOES NOT TAKE MUCH TO BE A HAMMER.

This might work with metal and wood but not so well in life. We tend to pound on people with bad language and name-calling because we do not have the right tools in our toolbox or have not developed the necessary skill sets to properly address important issues. Ecclesiastes 10:10 says, "If the ax is dull and its edge unsharpened, more strength is needed but skill will bring success." It takes skill and grace to communicate, but it does not take much to be a hammer.

takeaway

How would you describe your communication style? What are the areas in which you can improve?

reflect

_____

_____

_____

_____

_____

_____

_____

_____

_____

_____

_____

_____

⏱ minute 6

MARRIAGE

When my wife and I were married, we were so in love. We expected the fairy tale, but instead, it seemed like the beginning of a nuclear war. We were both convinced God had us fall in love to punish us for sins future and past. She did not live up to my expectations. I did not meet hers. I responded by constantly criticizing her, and she responded by nagging and withholding affection. The vicious cycle spun out of control until we realized a vital truth: we were in the same boat, and if we wanted to survive, we both needed to bail water. It finally dawned on me that if she lost, I lost. She began to realize my loss was her loss. We decided to change our mindsets. Instead of always trying to win, both of us began to make sure the other person was always the winner.

This little change caused our marriage to take on a strength that has endured 25 years. It was no longer about what I wanted from her but what I wanted for her, and vice versa. This unlocked the practical power of First Corinthians 13:5: "[Love] is not self-seeking, it is not easily angered, it keeps no record of wrongs." We discovered that love is simply looking for the win-win formula in every situation.

 **takeaway**

Recall a situation in your marriage or relationship in which you compromised and you both won.

reflect

_____

_____

_____

_____

_____

_____

_____

_____

_____

_____

_____

⏱ minute 7

KEEP IT DOWN

While I watched a famous Mafia movie, I noticed that when life-and-death decisions were made, the godfather did not shout, jump up and down, or even turn red. He usually spoke just above a whisper. I have noticed people who are really in charge do not have to go through a bunch of gyrations to get results. All they have to do is say the word.

IF YOU HAVE AUTHORITY, YOU DO NOT HAVE TO YELL.

In Matthew 8:8-9, a Roman soldier said to Jesus, "Lord, I do not deserve to have you come under my roof. But just say the word, and my servant will be healed. For I, myself, am a man under authority, with soldiers under me." In other words, the Roman soldier understood power. He didn't need to see a lightning bolt or feel the ground shake. He just needed the word spoken from someone who had the authority. This truth really hit home when the Lord spoke to me after getting frustrated with my two children. He said, "If you have authority, you do not have to yell." Oops.

 **takeaway**

Do you tend to use volume to accomplish effective communication? What was a time when you were able to accomplish more with a subdued demeanor?

reflect

_____

_____

_____

_____

_____

_____

_____

_____

_____

_____

_____

⏲ minute 8

LEADERSHIP & PARENTING

I am convinced parenting in the modern world is the most rigorous leadership test any human can undergo. One of the biggest mistakes new parents make is thinking their title equals power. By the time children become teenagers, parents begin to understand that only a track record of regard and earned respect can generate real influence in the lives of their children.

ONE OF THE BIGGEST MISTAKES NEW PARENTS MAKE IS THINKING THEIR TITLE EQUALS POWER.

One of the best ways to determine if you are parenting well is to ask yourself, "Do my children obey me because they have to or because they want to?" Remember, they will only "have to" until they are eighteen. They will spend the rest of their lives living out their "want to's." We have to learn to do more than just spank their behinds; we must also connect with their hearts and minds. Proverbs 22:6 says, "Train a child in the way he should go, and when he is old he will not turn from it" (KJV).

 **takeaway**

What are several ways in which you can connect with the hearts and minds of your children?

reflect

_____

_____

_____

_____

_____

_____

_____

_____

_____

_____

_____

⏰ minute 9

INSANITY

A common definition of *insanity* is "doing the same thing over and over again and expecting different results." Using this definition, most of us would have to admit that we all are sometimes a little bit crazy. We say the same things. We do the same things and go to the same places, yet somehow we expect things to change. But change doesn't happen until we do something new. Matthew 4:17 states, "Jesus began to preach, 'Repent, for the kingdom of heaven is near.'" The term *repent* simply means "to change." Christ's message was summed up in one word: *change*. In essence, He was saying, "Those who do not embrace change cannot become my followers."

CHANGE DOESN'T HAPPEN UNTIL WE DO SOMETHING NEW.

So let's become a little more open to change. Instead of telling our loved ones about all the things they don't do, let's tell them how much we love and need them. Instead of fussing with that child, take him or her out for a pizza, and remind yourself of the pleasure of sharing a good laugh. Maybe the people around you will change, if you change first.

 **takeaway**

What patterns of "insanity" do you observe in your own life, and how can you be more open to change?

💬 reflect

_____

_____

_____

_____

_____

_____

_____

_____

_____

_____

_____

🕙 minute 10

A JOSEPH

Matthew 1:18 says, "This is how the birth of Jesus came about: His mother Mary was pledged to be married to Joseph, but before they came together, she was found to be with child of the Holy Spirit."

I wonder why some people have so much trouble with this passage. If we can believe God created the universe out of nothing and created Adam from the dirt, what is the stretch in believing God would miraculously conceive Himself in a human womb? God is God, isn't He? God was painstaking in making it clear in the biblical record that no male was involved in the incarnation. But when it came to raising Jesus, God absolutely refused to let Mary raise Him without a man to father Him. An angel appeared to Joseph in a dream and said, "Don't be afraid to take Mary home with you as your wife, for what is conceived in her is from the Holy Spirit" (Matthew 1:20).

It takes both a male and a female to accomplish God's purposes in our children's lives. If Jesus needed a male role model, how much more do our children need male role models today? Perhaps you are not married to your child's father and can't think of one male who would be interested in mentoring your child. But remember, God still knows how to give dreams to men like Joseph.

 **takeaway**

Identify several specific ways in which you can pursue mentoring a child in your life.

💬 **reflect**

_____

_____

_____

_____

_____

_____

_____

_____

_____

_____

_____

_____

⏲ minute 11

NOT-TO-DO LIST

The first thing I do when I get to my office in the morning is write my "things to do" list. It helps keep me on track for the day. However, as my responsibilities have grown, I have learned that I need not only create my "to do" list, I also need a "not to do" list. This is also true at home.

- Item #1: Don't answer my wife too quickly when she talks to me. Listen first. Then speak.

- Item #2: Don't comment so much about petty things. Give my sons more space.

- Item #3: Stop eating so much junk food for lunch. How about eating more lunches that contain some broccoli, spinach, or cabbage?

This sounds really basic, but the concept has changed my life. Remember, most of the Ten Commandments begin with "Thou shalt not." So remember to balance your "things to do" list with a "things not to do" list. The results will amaze you.

 **takeaway**

Identify three items that should be added to your daily "not-to-do" list.

reflect

_____

_____

_____

_____

_____

_____

_____

_____

_____

_____

_____

_____

_____

⏱ minute 12

INVENTORY

Once a year, warehouses shut down to take inventory so that they can find out the difference between what the accounting records say is in stock and what is actually on the shelves. Almost always, the warehouse has less than what is on paper.

SOMETIMES WE ARE NOT LEGENDS IN OUR OWN TIME AS MUCH AS LEGENDS IN OUR OWN MINDS.

I have had times in my life when, like the business owner, I thought I had more on my shelves than I actually did. We tend to think that we are more kind, patient, and spiritual than we actually are. Second Corinthians 13:5 states, "Examine yourselves to see whether you are in the faith; test yourselves." In other words, take a personal inventory. Sometimes we are not legends in our own time as much as legends in our own minds. At least once a year we should ask the people we love, "Do I make you feel that you are valuable to me? Have I been patient with you?" And so on. You might be surprised by the answers, but get over it—and restock your shelves with what you need to be.

takeaway

As you take personal spiritual inventory, in what areas do you need to "restock your shelves"?

reflect

_____

_____

_____

_____

_____

_____

_____

_____

_____

_____

_____

_____

DOGS & CANS

I once heard a person on television tell a story about some mischievous boys and a stray dog. The boys had nothing to do, so they tied a string of cans around the dog's collar. The dog walked off at first, but the louder the noise of the dragging cans, the faster he ran. Hours later, the boys found the dog motionless and exhausted, lying on a neighborhood lawn.

BEFORE YOU POINT THE FINGER AT ANOTHER'S CANS AND CANNOTS, MAKE SURE YOU HAVE STOPPED RUNNING FROM YOUR OWN.

Often, we go from job to job, church to church, and relationship to relationship, not realizing that what we are running from is attached to us. Jesus said in Matthew 7:4–5, "How can you say to your brother, 'Let me take the speck out of your eye,' when all the time there is a plank in your own eye? . . . first take the plank out of your own eye, and then you will see clearly to remove the speck from your brother's eye." Before you point the finger at another's *cans* and *cannots*, make sure you have stopped running from your own.

 **takeaway**

What are several cans and cannots that you may be running from that hinder you from achieving greatness?

💬 **reflect**

_____

_____

_____

_____

_____

_____

_____

_____

_____

_____

_____

⏱ minute 14

COMMUNICATION, SEX, & MONEY

Relationship experts say that communication, sex, and money are the three greatest areas of struggle in most relationships. But, like a tripod with missing legs, many people think that sex and money are outside their heavenly Father's purview. The Bible says more about sex and money than most other subjects. You have heard it said, "What you do not know won't hurt you." Hosea 4:6 states, "My people are destroyed from lack of knowledge."

MANY PEOPLE THINK THAT SEX AND MONEY ARE OUTSIDE THEIR HEAVENLY FATHER'S PURVIEW.

The truth is, what you do not know is destroying you. No one can be expected to know more about a product than the manufacturer. If things are not working for you in your life, it is probably because you are not following the manufacturer's instruction manual. This Sunday around eleven o'clock in the morning, pull yourself into a shop and let a manufacturer's authorized dealer look under the hood. Remember, as with most products, if you do not use an authorized agent it will void the warranty. Get your oil change and let them replace your filters and fill you up with the fuel you need to be successful in life.

 **takeaway**

What areas of your life have you mistakenly considered outside your heavenly Father's purview?

reflect

_____

_____

_____

_____

_____

_____

_____

_____

_____

_____

_____

_____

⏱ minute 15

SUCCESS

One of the most important decisions you will make in life is determining your definition of success. It is the internal measuring rod of our self-worth, our level of personal satisfaction, and the guideline of all our dreams. How we characterize success is supremely important. Even the person who makes it his or her goal to be the most useless person in the world would have to decide what it means to be successfully useless. In our world, success is often measured by the titles we hold and the things we obtain. When I turned forty, I had met most of my life's goals but still had a nagging feeling of failure. I had to do some soul-searching. I took a closer look at the life of Jesus for help.

HOW WE CHARACTERIZE SUCCESS IS SUPREMELY IMPORTANT.

After He left His carpentry business, He lived on the charity of His followers. Isaiah 53:3 states that He was "despised and rejected of men." But today He is one of the most influential individuals who ever lived. I discovered that true success is not always in the accolades or the size of the mountains we climb. Success is ultimately measured by how much better we have helped make the lives of others.

 **takeaway**

What are several areas in which God has blessed you that you can leverage to invest in others?

reflect

_____

_____

_____

_____

_____

_____

_____

_____

_____

_____

_____

_____

section 3
FINANCES

⏱ minute 16

80/20 RULE

A fad spikes quickly but tends to fade just as fast. A positive trend, on the other hand, has a slow but steady rise. Today, there is much teaching about prosperity, using catchy slogans and novel ideas, but if we are wise, we will avoid the quick fixes and extremes and focus on establishing habits that will make a difference in the long term. Years ago, I began to live by the 80/20 rule. I learned to first invest my tithe into God's economy and then invest the next 10 percent into my savings and investments. I made it a rule to live off no more than 80 percent of my income. This one decision has radically changed my financial destiny. You might say, "I can't afford to do such a thing." The truth is you can't afford not to. If you live off 100 percent of your income, what are you going to do if something unexpected arises? When you give the first 10 percent to God, He promises to stretch the remaining 90 percent into more than you would have had if you kept 100 percent. When it comes to saving, you may need to start with only 1 percent of your income at first—but get started. Proverbs 13:11 states, "He who gathers money little by little makes it grow." If you are faithful, it will only be a matter of time before your money is working for you instead of you working for your money.

 **takeaway**

What is currently stopping you from living by the 80/20 rule in managing your finances?

reflect

_____

_____

_____

_____

_____

_____

_____

_____

_____

_____

_____

_____

⏱ minute 17

BLING

In Matthew 13:44, Jesus used this parable to teach his people about how to conduct business: "The kingdom of heaven is like treasure hidden in a field. When a man found it, he hid it again, and then in his joy he went and sold all he had and bought that field." Jesus was illustrating that sharp investors are always looking for undervalued purchases. Their motto is *buy low and sell high*.

THERE IS A BIG DIFFERENCE BETWEEN LOOKING PROSPEROUS AND BEING PROSPEROUS.

Most cars, clothing, and furniture are depreciating assets. We buy at high prices but have to sell them at low prices. On the other hand, an appreciating asset is something that gains value over time. The investor in the parable understood the value of obtaining an appreciating asset. He sold all his depreciating assets and invested the profits into the property that he secretly knew was undervalued. If we are going to be successful financially, it is important to learn that there is a big difference between looking prosperous and being prosperous. We may have to make some hard choices and postpone or even sell off a little bling so in the long run, we can establish the real thing, financial independence.

 **takeaway**

What are several examples from your own life of depreciating assets that you may be able to liquidate in order to invest in appreciating assets?

reflect

_____

_____

_____

_____

_____

_____

_____

_____

_____

_____

_____

MANAGEMENT

Genesis teaches that when God created man, the first thing He did was put him in the Garden of Eden to manage it. God would not ask Adam to do something that he did not have the ability to do. Obviously, innate in the makeup of humankind is the capacity to manage God's creation. In fact, much of life boils down to management. To have successful relationships, we must learn to manage conflict. If we are going to be successful on the job, we must learn to manage our priorities. What we manage well will grow, but whatever we mismanage, we will eventually lose. This is true with every area of life.

WHATEVER WE MISMANAGE, WE WILL EVENTUALLY LOSE.

Jesus says in Matthew 25:29, "Everyone who has will be given more, and he will have abundance. Whoever does not have, even what he has will be taken from him." Maybe our prayer should not be for God to give us more but for us to learn to manage better what we already have.

 takeaway

Identify several areas of your life that could be better managed and what it will take to prioritize them.

reflect

_____

_____

_____

_____

_____

_____

_____

_____

_____

_____

_____

_____

_____

⏰ minute 19

GOD & MONEY

Jesus said, "You cannot serve both God and money" (Matthew 6:24). Notice that He did not say that you cannot love God and *have* money. He warned against loving money and still trying to pretend that you worship God.

True worship has little to do with church buildings and liturgies. Worship is really about priorities. Jesus said to His followers, "Seek first his kingdom and his righteousness, and all these things will be given to you as well" (Matthew 6:33).

WORSHIP IS REALLY ABOUT PRIORITIES.

If you think about it, the thing that makes God truly God is not the fact that He is holy, loving, and righteous, although we are thankful for these attributes. It is the fact that He was first. Whatever we seek first in our lives has the ultimate position. God understands this and takes us through seasons in which we must make hard financial choices about what we will make or keep as our priority. Through this process He proves the genuineness of our faith. Always remember, where your treasure is your heart will be also. God does not need our money, but He does require our heart.

 **takeaway**

If you look at your financial priorities, what do they reveal about your worship priorities?

reflect

_____

_____

_____

_____

_____

_____

_____

_____

_____

_____

_____

_____

section 4
PROCESS

⊙ minute 20

RATS

A friend of mine once told me about a scientist who wanted to prove the power of hope. He put rats in a dish of water with sides too high to climb and water too deep to stand in. The rats could only swim. However, after a few minutes, the rats stopped swimming and drowned. The scientist decided to remove one of the rats from the dish when it stopped swimming (but before it actually drowned) and later subjected it to the same experiment with a fresh set of rats. He found that the rat did not drown in a few minutes like the rest but swam for more than twenty-four hours.

→ SOMETIMES GOD DELIVERS US AFTER ONLY MINUTES, AND OTHER TIMES DELIVERANCE COMES IN DAYS OR YEARS.

What transformed this rat? The fact that it had been saved before gave it hope that it would happen again. Sometimes God delivers us after only minutes, and other times deliverance comes in days or years. Why? Is it because He loses His love for us, or because He is the God who understands the necessity of building the spiritual muscle called hope? Romans 15:13 says, "May the God of hope fill you with all joy and peace as you trust in him."

 **takeaway**

Identify a time in which in hope gave you the power to endure a significant adversity?

reflect

_____

_____

_____

_____

_____

_____

_____

_____

_____

_____

_____

⏱ minute 21

WHAT IS PEACE?

The ancient philosopher Seneca made the observation, "The mind is never right but when it is at peace within itself."[4] But what is peace? It is the ability to stay in one piece when pressure tempts you to fall apart. Peace is having an inward grip on heaven when you are going through what feels like hell.

PEACE IS HAVING AN INWARD GRIP ON HEAVEN WHEN YOU ARE GOING THROUGH WHAT FEELS LIKE HELL.

Ultimately, peace is like having a Seeing Eye dog. It comes from a heart that has learned to trust even when it cannot see. Jesus said, "Peace I leave with you; my peace I give you. I do not give to you as the world gives" (John 14:27). The mind is never really right but when we learn to trust God.

 **takeaway**

What are several areas in which you need to find and apply the peace of God?

reflect

_____

_____

_____

_____

_____

_____

_____

_____

_____

_____

_____

_____

WORKING YOUR ROCK

There was a sickly, unemployed man who was a month behind in his mortgage. He looked out his front door and found that a two-ton rock had fallen out of the sky onto his lawn. He did not have the money to have it hauled away, so every morning he chiseled the rock with a hammer and wheeled the rock chips into his backyard.

BUT GOD DOES NOT WORK FOR THOSE WHO WILL NOT WORK FOR THEMSELVES.

After a week his skin was tanned. The second week he was able to work on the rock for hours at a time. By the end of the month his vigor came back. By the end of the second month his muscles were ripped and he was ready to take on the world again. A neighbor stopped by who happened to own a rock quarry and offered him fifty cents a pound for the rock chips, as well as a job. The money was enough to catch up on his mortgage with a little left over.

Romans 8:28 says, "God causes all things to work together for good to those who love God" (NAS). But God does not work for those who will not work for themselves. where ~ this ~ the word?

 **takeaway**

How has God used an adverse situation in your life toward your greater good?

reflect

_____

_____

_____

_____

_____

_____

_____

_____

_____

_____

_____

_____

⏱ minute 23

FAILURE AND SUCCESS

Failure is a vital part of success. If you have never failed, you have probably never tried anything of value. The great basketball icon Michael Jordan said, "I've missed more than nine thousand shots in my career. I've lost almost three hundred games. Twenty-six times, I've been trusted to take the game-winning shot and missed. I've failed over and over and over again in my life. And that is why I succeed."[5]

GOD IS NOT LOOKING FOR PEOPLE WHO HAVE NEVER FAILED.

One day, Jesus turned and looked at one of His disciples and said, "Simon, Simon, Satan has asked to sift you as wheat, but I have prayed for you, Simon, that your faith may not fail" (Luke 22:31-32). Simon responded by saying that he would never betray Jesus, but hours later he did just that. Most would expect Him to have given up on such a wishy-washy disciple, but God is not looking for people who have never failed. Instead, He is looking for people who refuse to quit and stay down after they have been knocked down. Failure only becomes fatal when you stop getting get back up again.

 **takeaway**

How have you historically dealt with failure in your life—by getting up or staying down?

reflect

_____

_____

_____

_____

_____

_____

_____

_____

_____

_____

GRASS IS ALWAYS GREENER

You have heard the expression that the grass is always greener on the other side. The reason the grass is so green is because the people on the other side have had to walk through a bunch of cow dung. If you want to accomplish anything of value, you are going to have to go through some crap. No one arrives at the top without a story to tell.

NO ONE ARRIVES AT THE TOP WITHOUT A STORY TO TELL.

If you let the manure do its fertilizing, it won't be long before what was intended for evil begins to work for your good. In the end it will develop a strength that will make you vibrant and strong. Proverbs 14:4 states, "Where no oxen are, the manger is clean" (NAS). Remember, the ox was the largest work animal in the Middle East. The only time there are no piles of mess is when there is no ox and the manger is clean. When the manger is clean, nothing is getting done. If you want to make any progress, you will have to get used to using a shovel.

Remember the words of Frederick Douglass: "If there is no struggle, there is no progress."[6]

 **takeaway**

How have you seen God working in the messiness of your life?

💭 **reflect**

_____

_____

_____

_____

_____

_____

_____

_____

_____

_____

_____

_____

_____

section 5
PREPARATION

⏱ minute 25

NO "I"

The natural progression of things is that we are taught before we teach, we rent before we own, and we live under our parents' rules before we can make our own. Jesus said, in Luke 16:12, "If you have not been trustworthy with someone else's property, who will give you property of your own?" The greatest test of character is not how well we advance our own interests but how willing we are to advance the interests of others. If we learn to make others look good, become agreeable to someone else's way of doing things, or help someone else fulfill his or her vision, we will discover that whatever we make happen for others, God will make happen for us.

THE GREATEST TEST OF CHARACTER IS NOT HOW WELL WE ADVANCE OUR OWN INTERESTS BUT HOW WILLING WE ARE TO ADVANCE THE INTERESTS OF OTHERS.

Sometimes promotions are withheld not because of our aptitude but because of our attitude. You have heard it said that there is no *I* in the word *team*. So get over yourself and help someone else. It might be counter-intuitive, but we become most valuable when we add value to others.

takeaway

Identify several people whose interests you could help advance and how you would do so.

reflect

_____

_____

_____

_____

_____

_____

_____

_____

_____

_____

_____

_____

COMPLACENCY

Seafarers say that the most dangerous time at sea is when the waters are calm. When the sun is out and the ocean is smooth, sailors tend to walk farther from the railing and are less careful about their footing.

Storms on the seas are often sudden, and if you are not vigilant at all times, you could very easily be tossed overboard.

THE MOST DANGEROUS TIMES IN OUR LIVES ARE NOT IN THE MIDDLE OF A STORM

Likewise, the most dangerous times in our lives are not in the middle of a storm but typically right after our victories. In these moments, we tend to bask in the glory of our most recent achievement and start to let down our guard. First Corinthians 10:12 states, "If you think you are standing firm, be careful that you don't fall!" Are you still holding on tightly to God, or have you become a little overconfident? If yesterday's achievements have become your finish line, you too are finished. Stay connected, stay ready, and always be fired up about the possibilities ahead.

 **takeaway**

In what areas of your life can you identify complacency and overconfidence that could spell danger in the future?

reflect

_____

_____

_____

_____

_____

_____

_____

_____

_____

_____

COACH

The other day, I tried to teach my son how to improve his jump shot. I showed him that a jump shot had to be taken with his wrists above his head if he was going to use his height to his advantage. Then I went inside the house. A half hour later, my son came into the house mad because he was not able to make the shot using the new form. In my typical-dad manner, I said, "Okay, then let people keep blocking your shot."

IF WE WANT TO SUCCEED, WE MUST REMAIN COACHABLE.

I am not a professional basketball player, but I am sure that I know enough to help a fifth grader play better. James 1:21 says, "Humbly accept the word planted in you, which can save you." If we do not learn to receive training from those with a little more experience than we have, we will keep having our shots blocked in life.

If we want to succeed, we must remain coachable. The power to learn is directly affected by our willingness to accept good advice.

 **takeaway**

Identify several areas of weakness in your life that could benefit from the wisdom of a coach—then get some coaching!

reflect

_____

_____

_____

_____

_____

_____

_____

_____

_____

_____

_____

SEASONS

Abraham Lincoln said, "If I had eight hours to chop down a tree, I'd spend six hours sharpening my ax."[7] Jesus spent thirty years of His life preparing for only three years of ministry. Sometimes we are in such a hurry, we forget that what goes up fast usually comes down just as fast.

Before you make another New Year's resolution, let's consider the words of Solomon.

WHAT GOES UP FAST USUALLY COMES DOWN JUST AS FAST.

There is a time for everything... a time to be born and a time to die, a time to plant and a time to uproot, a time to kill and a time to heal, a time to tear down and a time to build, a time to weep and a time to laugh, a time to mourn and a time to dance... a time to search and a time to give up, a time to keep and a time to throw away, a time to tear and a time to mend, a time to be silent and a time to speak. (Ecclesiastes 3:1–4 & 6–7)

Let's not try to have a harvest when it is our season to plant. Knowing which season you are in in your life may spare you a lot of heartache and disappointment.

takeaway

Are you in a season of "axe sharpening" or a season in which you should be applying what you have prepared for?

reflect

_____

_____

_____

_____

_____

_____

_____

_____

_____

_____

section 6
ATONEMENT

THE TEN COMMANDMENTS

A man cheated on his taxes and was caught by the government. His defense was, "Everyone else does it, so why should I be fined?" Not only was he fined, but he was put in jail.

THE FACT THAT EVERYONE ELSE HAS ALSO BROKEN THE LAW DOES NOT CHANGE THE COMMANDMENT.

The Ten Commandments state, Thou shall not lie. Thou shall not commit adultery. Thou shall not lust after your neighbor's house or spouse, and the list goes on. If you have ever lied, cheated, or lusted, in the eyes of the law you are a liar, a cheater, and a pervert. The fact that everyone else has also broken the law does not change the commandment. The good news is that if we throw ourselves on the mercy of the court and admit our missteps, Jesus is willing to take our case before God. First Timothy 2:5 states, "For there is one God and one mediator between God and men, the man Christ Jesus." Jesus has never lost a case. But you must confess before He can bless.

 takeaway

What are the areas of sin or weakness in your life that you should confess and deal with?

💬 reflect

_____

_____

_____

_____

_____

_____

_____

_____

_____

_____

_____

_____

BELL TOWER

The British had a tradition of hanging convicted criminals when the bell tolled at eight o'clock in the morning. One day, a convicted felon was escorted to the platform. A white hood was placed over his head, and the executioner waited for the bell to ring.

At eight o'clock, the bell rope was pulled, but there was no sound. It was pulled again and then again. Soon, droplets of blood dripped from the bell onto the man who pulled the rope. He looked up to see what was happening and saw that a man had wrapped his body around the fifty-pound gong of the bell and had kept the bell from ringing.

The convicted man's younger brother had climbed the bell tower to keep the bell from tolling. The executioner and the crowd were silenced by the sight. They decided that one death was enough for the day and allowed the convicted man to go free. Jesus has climbed your bell tower. John 8:36 says, "If the Son sets you free, you will be free indeed."

 **takeaway**

What are the areas of your life that you still need to seek God for freedom from?

reflect

_____

_____

_____

_____

_____

_____

_____

_____

_____

_____

_____

_____

THE MEASURE OF A KING

The English needed to standardize their units of measurement. They decided to determine the length of a yard by measuring the distance between King Henry I's nose and thumb.

THE STATEMENT "JESUS IS LORD" IS MORE THAN A CATCHPHRASE.

Today, many are saying, "I do not need all that Jesus stuff. After all, I am not as bad as the next guy." Paul comments, "When we measure ourselves by ourselves and compare ourselves with ourselves, we are not wise." (Second Corinthians 10:12) When we compare our faults with those of other mortals, we tend to walk away feeling justified. However, if Jesus is the immortal King, His life should be the ultimate standard of measurement. The question is not how you line up against your neighbor but how well you have aligned yourself with Christ.

The statement "Jesus is Lord" is more than a catchphrase. It is a statement demonstrated in our lifestyle and measured by the length of our willingness to obey.

 **takeaway**

Are there parts of your life over which you have yet to declare Jesus as Lord?

reflect

_____

_____

_____

_____

_____

_____

_____

_____

_____

_____

_____

_____

minute 32

THE GREAT EXCHANGE

Have you ever handed a cashier a ten-dollar bill, only to be given change as if you had given just a dollar? Did you complain? If he or she refused to correct the situation, did you promise never to go back to that store?

SOMETIMES WE TRY TO SHORTCHANGE GOD AND WONDER WHY HE SEEMS SO DISTANT.

Following Christ has been called the great exchange. We meet God at the cross and exchange our faults for His mercy. But the requirement is simple—all of us, for all of Him. Sometimes we try to shortchange God and wonder why He seems so distant. Jeremiah 29:13 states, "You will seek me and find me when you seek me with all your heart." If you want to be successful in your walk with God, it is an all-or-nothing proposition.

 **takeaway**

What is it in your life that causes you to feel distant from God, and what can you do to bring intimacy to your relationship with Him?

reflect

_____

_____

_____

_____

_____

_____

_____

_____

_____

_____

_____

THE NAKED TRUTH

Before I became a believer, I spent hours studying the world's major religions and philosophies in the hope of finding the truth. Christian friends told me that I did not need to understand the Bible, only believe it. I was relieved when I discovered that the Bible taught otherwise. First Peter 3:15 says, "Always be prepared to give an answer to everyone who asks you to give the reason for the hope that you have." It wasn't until someone was prepared to explain the Scriptures to me that I could believe them.

I heard this story around that time in my life: One day Truth undressed to go swimming. While Truth was swimming, Lie stole his clothes. Then Lie put on Truth's clothes and visited the nearest town. For hours, Lie masqueraded as Truth until, eventually, the sheriff told his deputy to arrest Lie. The townspeople said, "Why should we arrest that man?" The sheriff said, "Because I can see the naked Truth running up the hill."

Sometimes people are confused, not because they do not want to believe but because no one has had the patience to point out the naked Truth.

 **takeaway**

What are some lies that you used to believe, and what is the truth that has replaced them?

reflect

_____

_____

_____

_____

_____

_____

_____

_____

_____

_____

_____

section 7
ASSOCIATIONS

A LESSON FROM GEESE

I do not need a prophetic gift to predict where you will be in five years. Anyone can forecast your tomorrow by looking at the people you hang around today. First Corinthians 15:33 says, "Do not be misled: 'Bad company corrupts good character.'" Imagine what good company might do!

ANYONE CAN FORECAST YOUR TOMORROW BY LOOKING AT THE PEOPLE YOU HANG AROUND TODAY.

Many people have questioned the importance of becoming part of a church. I think the answer can be illustrated in nature. I have read that when geese form the V formation, the whole flock adds over 70 percent to its flying range. When each bird flaps its wings, it becomes uplift for the birds that are following.

Please don't mishear me. Don't just join any church, but find a church where you experience uplift. Find a church that flies in divine order, and then don't just sit and stare—connect your gifts and talents to the formation.

takeaway

How are the relationships in your life advancing or impeding your success?

reflect

_____

_____

_____

_____

_____

_____

_____

_____

_____

_____

_____

_____

THE MINISTRY

When the subject of preachers comes up at the Thanksgiving table, watch out. At least one member of the family is going to have a personal experience with abuse while the rest are going to give examples of a preacher having a house that is too big or a car that is too expensive. Often the criticism is well deserved, but what concerns me is the idea that ministers are held to a higher standard than others. This idea is dangerous.

THE NEXT TIME YOU CRITICIZE THE CLERGY, MAKE SURE YOU ARE HOLDING HIM OR HER TO THE SAME STANDARD AS YOU WOULD YOURSELF

There is only one standard for all men. Ministers don't read a different Bible.

James 3:1 states, "Not many of you should presume to be teachers, my brothers, because you know that we who teach will be judged more strictly." Preachers do not have a different standard but a stricter judgment based on the same standard. The next time you criticize the clergy, make sure you are holding him or her to the same standard as you would yourself—and let God alone be the judge for anything beyond that.

 **takeaway**

In what ways do you hold others to higher standards than yourself—overlooking your own weaknesses?

reflect

_____

_____

_____

_____

_____

_____

_____

_____

_____

_____

_____

ADAM AND EVE

Right after Adam and Eve ate from the Tree of the Knowledge of Good and Evil in Genesis 3:9, the Lord called to the man and said, "Where are you?" Is it that God did not know where Adam was? God asked the question not because He could not find Adam but to help Adam find himself.

Everyone needs at least one person in his or her life who is allowed to ask the hard questions: "Where are you now? Are you hiding behind mistakes or are you facing them? Are you shifting responsibility and making your past another excuse for why you no longer try?"

EVERYONE NEEDS AT LEAST ONE PERSON IN HIS OR HER LIFE WHO IS ALLOWED TO ASK THE HARD QUESTIONS.

Instead of the Lord having to hunt you down and ask, "Where are you?" why not take the initiative and say, "Lord, here I am, faults, blemishes, and all. I have no excuses and no one else to blame. All I ask for is Your mercy and grace to do better." This is a very simple prayer, but it often gets profound results.

 **takeaway**

What are some of your hidden faults and sins, and what excuses are you making for them, rather than bringing them to God?

reflect

_____

_____

_____

_____

_____

_____

_____

_____

_____

_____

FRIENDS & CHICKENS

Jesus said to a group of fishermen, "Come follow me and I will make you fishers of men" (Mark 1:17). The promise was simple. If they followed, Jesus would make them fishers of men. The law of association states that you will become like the top five people you most closely associate with. In other words, if you want to know where you are going to end up in life, take a look at your closest associates.

IF YOU WANT TO KNOW WHERE YOU ARE GOING TO END UP IN LIFE, TAKE A LOOK AT YOUR CLOSEST ASSOCIATES.

This law so affected Christ's disciples that Acts 4:13 states, "When they saw the courage of Peter and John and realized that they were unschooled, ordinary men, they were astonished and they took note that these men had been with Jesus." Over time, Jesus had rubbed off on them. The term *anointing* literally means "rubbed-on oil." If you want to increase the anointing in your life, you just need to upgrade those you rub shoulders with. You will never soar like an eagle if you continue pecking with chickens.

 **takeaway**

What are some relationships you can cultivate that will allow you to be "rubbed off" on in a positive way?

reflect

_____

_____

_____

_____

_____

_____

_____

_____

_____

_____

_____

_____

section 8
WISDOM

GET A HANDLE

Have you ever picked up a steaming-hot coffee cup without using the handle? Man, it burns. Handles are designed to help diffuse the heat so we can safely pick up a hot cup.

Sometimes situations in life get heated, but God has provided us with handles to keep us from getting burned. Proverbs 15:1 is one such handle: "A gentle answer turns away wrath, but a harsh word stirs up anger."

YOU CAN CATCH MORE FLIES WITH HONEY THAN VINEGAR.

Have you ever noticed that it takes two to fight? My wife learned this years ago. When I would get angry, she would respond by being sweet. She understood that I could not have an argument by myself.

The next time someone goes off on you, pause and get a handle on yourself. Remember, you can catch more flies with honey than vinegar.

 **takeaway**

Recall an incident in which you learned to respond to anger with a "gentle answer."

reflect

_____

_____

_____

_____

_____

_____

_____

_____

_____

_____

_____

THE POWER OF THE TONGUE

Years ago, something painful happened to me. It was totally unexpected, and I was deeply wounded. No matter what I did, I could not get the thing off my mind. And the more I talked about it, the more it seemed to fester. Proverbs 18:21 states, "The tongue has the power of life and death." I did not realize that each time I spoke bitterly about the situation, I was peeling back the scab and only delaying the healing process.

AFTER I TALK OR PRAY THROUGH A MATTER, I NEED TO BE QUIET ABOUT IT.

I have since learned that after I talk or pray through a matter, I need to let it go. I do not add logs to a fire that I wish would burn out. You can have life or death by what you choose to talk about or what you choose to stop talking about. The power is yours.

takeaway

What is a situation in your life that causes you pain but which you keep reflecting on or talking about? Resolve to release it.

reflect

_____

_____

_____

_____

_____

_____

_____

_____

_____

_____

⏰ minute 40

GET UNDERSTANDING

Helen Keller said of Philippians 4:7, "I do not want the peace which passeth understanding, I want the understanding which bringeth peace."[8] She misunderstood the Scripture, but she was on to something. Solomon says, "Though it cost all you have, get understanding" (Proverbs 4:7). I often hear people say, "I have done all I know to do, but nothing seems to work." But that statement belies the problem. You may have done all *you* know to do; the problem is sometimes that we just do not know enough. *interesting*

MIRACLES ARE GOD'S WAY OF CORRECTING THINGS THAT HAVE ALREADY GONE WRONG.

I have experienced life-altering miracles from God, and I am very grateful. But I have also found that if I operate with greater understanding, I will not need as many miracles. Before we ask God for our next miracle, maybe we should ask Him to give us greater wisdom about how we should conduct our affairs. In large measure, miracles are God's way of correcting things that have already gone wrong. But if we pursue wisdom, we can often intercept problems before they even happen.

 **takeaway**

Identify several areas of your life, work or ministry in which you need to "get understanding."

reflect

_____

_____

_____

_____

_____

_____

_____

_____

_____

_____

_____

HALT

Years ago, I received advice from a veteran of the faith. His advice has kept me anchored during very difficult moments. He said, "Whenever you are confronted by trying circumstances, remember the acronym HALT. Whenever you are 'hungry, angry, lonely, or tired,' do not make long-term decisions."[9]

OFTEN, A DELAYED RESPONSE IS BETTER THAN A BAD ONE.

I have learned that in such times, I had to apply the "twenty-four-hour rule;" it is wise to give myself twenty-four hours to gain perspective. If I do this, it gives me a chance to gain perspective and not to speak out of my hurt, but what is best for the situation. Ephesians 4:29 says, "Do not let any unwholesome talk come out of your mouths, but only what is helpful for building others up according to their needs, that it may benefit those who listen."

When we are hungry, angry, lonely, or tired, our personal deficit tends to distort reality, and we begin to see our concerns as primary and the needs of others as secondary. Our response must not only benefit ourselves, but our first concern must be the benefit of the listener. Often, a delayed response is better than a bad one.

 **takeaway**

Recall a time when you did not follow the acronym HALT. What were the results?

reflect

_____

_____

_____

_____

_____

_____

_____

_____

_____

_____

_____

section 9
CHARACTER

GUARD YOUR HEART

It does not take a lot of skill to tear down a fence, but it does take a lot of hard work to put one up. If you are going to attempt something worthwhile in life, it is important to learn to tune certain people out. The first thing I do whenever I am criticized is consider the source. Is the critic qualified? Have they ever been in my situation before? Then I rule out certain critiques.

CRITICISM IS ALWAYS AN OPPORTUNITY TO GROW.

The second thing I do is try to understand their motive. Do they care about me? It is not wise to lose sleep thinking about the opinions of people who would not cry at my funeral.

Lastly, I have to guard against becoming so offended that I cannot look for the kernel of truth. Criticism is always an opportunity to grow. So keep your heart and words sweet, because if your critic is right, you may have to eat them. Proverbs 4:23 states, "Above all else, guard the response of your heart." If you don't guard your heart, no one else will.

takeaway

Recall a time when you were able to learn and grow from a critic's feedback.

💬 reflect

_____

_____

_____

_____

_____

_____

_____

_____

_____

_____

_____

_____

KEEPING MYSELF HONEST

I had a jogging buddy who was on a diet. I was not very supportive because he had been on a diet for as long as I'd known him. For a whole month, he would congratulate himself for eating three small meals a day, even though I could see his shorts getting tighter. At the end of the month, he asked me to get out my scale so he could weigh himself. He was ten pounds heavier. He was devastated. It is one thing to twist the truth for others, but it is far more painful when we lie to ourselves.

THE TRUTH WILL EVENTUALLY COME OUT.

We are all tempted to tell less than the truth at times. R. T. Kendall says, "A lie is merely the postponement of a truth that is eventually going to come out."[10] In Matthew 10:26, Jesus said it this way: "There is nothing concealed that will not be disclosed, or hidden that will not be made known." In other words, what we do in secret will be brought into the light. So why cause further embarrassment by postponing the inevitable? You can just say it or delay it. But the truth will eventually come out.

 **takeaway**

What are the areas of your life in which you face temptation to be less than honest—with yourself and others.

reflect

_____

_____

_____

_____

_____

_____

_____

_____

_____

_____

⏰ minute 44

WHAT DO YOUR CLOTHES SMELL LIKE?

I am not proud of this, but when I was a kid, I had my share of fistfights. Even the times I won, I was left with cuts and bruises that took time to heal. Second Corinthians 2:14 says, "Thanks be to God who always leads us in triumph in Christ" (NAS). God promises us that we will win, but sometimes it is not without a fight. In Acts 14, Paul was stoned. God prevailed, and His servant miraculously survived, but after the broken teeth, crushed bones, and the holes that the stones left in his body, he needed not only to survive but also to be healed.

You may have survived another week, but have you been healed? The book of Daniel tells us about three Hebrew boys who were thrown into the fire for obeying God but miraculously came out without the smell of smoke on their clothes. They not only survived, but they did so without the smell of bitterness, unforgiveness, or disgrace on their wardrobe. You may have survived, but what would people who are closest to you say your clothes smell like?

Thank you Lord!

 **takeaway**

Identify an area of your life in which you survived crisis, but may still need healing from bitterness, unforgiveness or disgrace.

reflect

_____

_____

_____

_____

_____

_____

_____

_____

_____

_____

_____

BIG LITTLE U IN MINISTRY

One day I was complaining to God about a situation that was difficult for me. After a great deal of patience, He responded, "The only thing I hurt was your pride." The letter "i" is conveniently placed in the middle of both words: *pride and sin*. We have to guard against our "i's" becoming the center of our lives.

SOMETIMES WE LET OUR "I"S BECOME THE CENTER OF OUR LIVES.

Philippians 2:3 says, "Do nothing out of selfish ambition or vain conceit, but in humility consider others better than yourselves." We cannot defeat the big *I* until we look at our loved ones and decide our first concern is *U*. It may not please an English teacher to write lowercase *i*'s and capital *U*s in an essay, but it would surely please God if we so punctuated our hearts.

 **takeaway**

How has pride—and "selfish ambition" damaged your ability to place the needs of others above your own?

reflect

_____

_____

_____

_____

_____

_____

_____

_____

_____

_____

_____

_____

⏰ minute 46

HUMILITY

Everything of value is imitated. It may look like the original, sound like the original, even smell like the original, but after closer inspection, at times we will discover that it is not what we had hoped. The same is true with ideals.

NEVER SUBTRACT FROM WHO GOD HAS CREATED YOU TO BE, TO BE DOWN WITH A CROWD.

I desperately wanted to be godly, so I naturally wanted to be humble. I did everything I could not to stand out. I would dumb down, dress down, and speak down— anything it took to fit in with those I wanted to be down with. Then I read a quote from St. Paul: "Do not let anyone who delights in false [pseudo] humility and the worship of angels disqualify you for the prize" (Colossians 2:18). Paul was saying that humility can be counterfeited. I think C. S. Lewis summed it up best, "Humility is not thinking less of yourself, but thinking of yourself less ."

Never subtract from who God has created you to be, to be down with a crowd. True humility not only recognizes our weaknesses but also acknowledges our strengths.

 **takeaway**

Identify a time when you acted in false-humility or pride to gain or keep the accolades of a crowd.

💬 **reflect**

_____

_____

_____

_____

_____

_____

_____

_____

_____

_____

_____

section 10
FAITH & FEAR

🕐 minute 47

DO NOT BE AFRAID

A scholar once stated that "Do not be afraid" in one form or another appears 365 times in the Bible, once for every day of the year. Although I've never counted for myself, I can imagine this is true. A common acronym for the word *fear* is "false evidence appearing real." We usually become afraid when we confuse facts (false evidence) with the truth.

EVEN THE FACTS HAVE TO SAY *AMEN.*

The fact may be that you are having some troubles in your relationships, but the biblical truth is, "Love never fails" (First Corinthians 13:8). The fact may be that you are sinking in debt, but the truth is, "If any of you lacks wisdom, let him ask of God, who gives to all liberally and without reproach" (James 1:5, NKJV).

The fact may be that you feel like giving up, but the truth is, "Having done everything to stand, stand firm" (Ephesians 6:13, NAS). Facts are only as big as our faith allows them to be. Faith is often sticking with the truth until it gets so big in our hearts that even the facts have to say *amen.*

 **takeaway**

What is an situation of "false evidence appearing real" in your life that needs to be confronted with faith?

reflect

_____

_____

_____

_____

_____

_____

_____

_____

_____

_____

_____

⏱ minute 48

TIMOTHY

Young Timothy was frightened. With every footstep he heard outside his door, he thought it might be Roman soldiers coming to arrest him. The persecution of the church under Emperor Nero had reached a fever pitch, and Timothy started to give out under the weight of it all.

WHAT GOD GIVES YOU, LET NO ONE TAKE AWAY.

Meanwhile, the apostle Paul, imprisoned in a cold dungeon awaiting his execution, wrote these life-changing words to Timothy: "God has not given us a spirit of fear, but a spirit of power and of love and of a sound mind" (Second Timothy 1:7, NKJV).

You might have expected Paul to be more sympathetic, but this was not what the young pastor really needed. Timothy needed to man up, square his shoulders, lift up his head, and know where his hope came from. Like you, I have had days when I have felt like finding a corner somewhere to crawl into and hide. But Scripture tells us that God did not give us a quitting, shrinking, or running-away spirit; He gave us a spirit of inexplicable inner strength, pure vision, and the ability to keep our head in the worst of situations. What God gives you, let no one take away.

 **takeaway**

Identify a time when God provided you with supernatural "power, love and sound mind" in the face of a crisis?

reflect

_____

_____

_____

_____

_____

_____

_____

_____

_____

_____

_____

⏱ minute 49

SEED

In 2005, scientists germinated a seed excavated from Herod the Great's palace in Israel. Although the seed was two thousand years old, it grew into a three-foot-tall plant.

Jesus taught, "The kingdom of heaven is like a... seed" (Matthew 13:31). A seed is something that holds tremendous potential but cannot grow until it is planted. Many people think that the message of God's kingdom is outdated, but just like King Herod's seed, if it gets planted in the heart, it has the same potential for miracles as it did two thousand years ago. After all, as Hebrews 13:8 says, "Jesus is the same yesterday and today and forever."

In my late twenties and early thirties, I suffered from a debilitating disease. After five surgeries, the doctors had given up and I was left with constant bleeding and intense daily pain. I had prayed for years with no success, until one day, after a time of prayer, I knew something in me was different. I returned to the doctor days later, and the doctor verified that I was completely healed. There was no natural explanation for the events except that Jesus, who healed the sick two thousand years ago, still heals today. His Word is like a seed; if you get it into your heart, it will grow.

 **takeaway**

What is a challenge in your life that you could address with the seed of the Word of God?

reflect

_____

_____

_____

_____

_____

_____

_____

_____

_____

_____

_____

CONSPIRACY THEORY

How many of us have heard that NASA faked the moon landing or that our government was behind the events of 9/11? We still hear of Elvis and Tupac sightings. A conspiracy theory is basically the belief that behind a major event is a deceptive plot by a secret and powerful group to advance their agenda.

GOD IS EVER PLANNING AND SCHEMING FOR OUR GOOD.

As a Washington, D.C., area pastor, who has spent hours counseling people involved in political intrigues, I understand that there is always a story behind the story. Jeremiah 29:11 states, "'For I know the plans I have for you,' declares the Lord, 'plans to prosper you and not to harm you, plans to give you hope and a future.'" According to Jeremiah, not only are our enemies conspiring, but so is God. He is ever planning and scheming for our good. The next time you are in a crisis, realize that the conspiracy to bless you is so much greater than any conspiracy to do you harm. God is on your side.

 **takeaway**

How have you seen God's "conspiracy for good" working in your life recently?

reflect

_____

_____

_____

_____

_____

_____

_____

_____

_____

_____

_____

_____

⏱ minute 51

MORE FAITH

I think the best description of the word *faith* is "trust." Trust is the quiet assurance that comes from knowing that a person or a thing will do what you expect. Paul says in Second Thessalonians 1:3, "We ought always to thank God for you, brothers, and rightly so, because your faith is growing more and more." How does faith grow? Trust, like faith, grows only with time and experience.

THE MORE TIME I INVEST IN GOD'S PRESENCE, THE EASIER IT IS FOR ME TO KNOW WHAT TO EXPECT.

Faith in people comes from interacting with them and discovering what we can expect from them. Because I spend so much time with my wife, when I pull into my driveway, I usually know what to expect. The same is true with God. The more time I invest in His presence, the easier it is for me to know what to expect. Sometimes we do not believe as we should, not because God is so hard to trust, but because we have invested so little time building our trust in Him. God, an open heart and time spent with Him equals much more faith.

 **takeaway**

What are several ways you can open your heart and spend time with God in order to grow your faith?

reflect

_____

_____

_____

_____

_____

_____

_____

_____

_____

_____

_____

_____

⏱ minute 52

A TURTLE'S FAITH

This morning I stepped off my front porch and almost put two hundred pounds and my hard-soled dress shoes on the back of a foot-long turtle. The turtle was as surprised as I was, but all he did was stick his neck back into his shell.

SOMETIMES THE GREATEST EXPRESSION OF FAITH IS WHEN WE WITHDRAW INTO THE SHELL OF THE WORD OF GOD

How could it be so calm? The turtle was at peace with the fact that it was not born with the speed to outrun trouble. Instead, it was given armor to withstand it. Psalm 119:114 states, "You are my refuge and my shield; I have put my hope in your word."

Sometimes the greatest expression of faith is when we withdraw into the shell of the Word of God and just trust. I have seen that turtle walk away from an 80-pound biting dog simply because it had the good sense to trust its shell. Has God provided more for turtles than for you and me? Ephesians 6:13 says, "Therefore put on the full armor of God, so that when the day of evil comes, you may be able to stand your ground."

takeaway

Recall a time when you were not able to respond to a challenge with anything other than trusting God to be your "refuge and shield."

reflect

_____

_____

_____

_____

_____

_____

_____

_____

_____

_____

section 11
SELF-ESTEEM

⏱ minute 53

WHAT YOU PUT UP WITH

Frederick Douglass offered some advice that has been a guide for me: "Power concedes nothing without a demand. It never did and it never will. Find out just what any people will quietly submit to and you have found out the exact amount of injustice and wrong which will be imposed upon them... The limits of tyrants are prescribed by the endurance of those whom they oppress."[11] In other words, no one can ride your back unless you bend over. So stop complaining about those who are trying to ride you and stand up.

NO ONE CAN RIDE YOUR BACK UNLESS YOU BEND OVER.

Jesus said in Matthew 16:19, "Whatever you forbid on earth will be forbidden in heaven, and whatever you permit on earth will be permitted in heaven." (NLT) Maybe your problem is not so much what a certain person is trying to do to you but what you are willing to put up with.

 **takeaway**

What is something that you are putting up with—and complaining about—that should be addressed?

reflect

_____

_____

_____

_____

_____

_____

_____

_____

_____

_____

_____

THE ENEMY WITHIN

An African proverb states, "If there is no enemy within, there is no enemy without." Jesus did not talk much about the Devil's operations outside of people's hearts. Why did Jesus not teach more on the subject? As long as Satan is on the outside of a person, he is not much of a threat. It is only when he enters our hearts through word, thought, or deed that he gains real power and control.

AS LONG AS SATAN IS ON THE OUTSIDE OF A PERSON, HE IS NOT MUCH OF A THREAT.

Satan tries everything in his power to stop God's plan for our lives, but as long as his work is only external, we have no reason to fear. Romans 8:38–39 exudes this confidence: "For I am convinced that neither death nor life, angels nor demons, the present nor the future, nor any powers, neither height nor depth, nor anything else in all creation, will be able to separate us from the love of God that is in Christ Jesus our Lord." Dealing with the Devil is a lot like a boat ride. As long as the water is outside the boat, it floats. However, if water gets inside the boat, you are sunk. The Devil may be in the world, but as long as he is not in our hearts, we can continue to rise above it all.

 **takeaway**

Identify an area of your life in which you have allowed the Devil to gain power and control.

reflect

_____

_____

_____

_____

_____

_____

_____

_____

_____

_____

_____

_____

(L) minute 55

NOTHING TO PROVE

God's introduction of Himself in Scripture does not begin with any explanations. Genesis 1:1 simply states, "In the beginning God…" As the song title says, "Whoomp! There it is!" Later, Moses is at the burning bush and asks God, "What is your name?" God's response is short: "I AM WHO I AM" (Exodus 3:14). In the New Testament, some people were arguing with Jesus about His identity, and Jesus settled it with one statement: "Most assuredly, I say to you, before Abraham was, I AM" (John 8:58, NKJV).

I AM, BECAUSE GOD CHOSE ME TO BE.

People may try to saddle you with arguments against who you are, where you came from, or what you can ultimately do. But you will never experience true freedom until you decide that you don't have to argue. When you start seeing your worth, you'll find it unnecessary to argue with people who don't.

takeaway

Make a list of the ways in which God has placed value in you that have no relation to where you came from or what you can do.

reflect

_____

_____

_____

_____

_____

_____

_____

_____

_____

_____

_____

⏱ minute 56

THE LION

My friend the late Dr. Myles Munroe once told this story.

A shepherd adopted a lost lion cub and let the lion join his flock of sheep. The lion learned to eat grass and even *baa* like the sheep. One day, the herd became agitated and started to panic. The lion asked, "Why is everyone so frightened?" The sheep told him that a vicious beast was just over the hill.

The cub peeked over the hill and saw the most frightening beast he had ever seen. The beast released the fiercest roar that the cub had ever heard. He was terrified and ran back to the safety of the herd, trembling.

Months later, he went to drink at a stream. As he drank, he saw the reflection of the beast. He let out the loudest scream he could, but what came out his mouth was a roar like the beast. It was scary, but it felt so good. Full of adrenaline, he felt his muscles tighten, and a confidence overcame him as he dared to go back to the water's edge to look again at the beast in the water. As he looked, the beast mirrored his every movement, and he realized for the first time that he was not a sheep but a lion.[13]

Many of us are *baa*-ing through life, when God has created us to roar. Proverbs 28:1 says, "But the righteous are as bold as a lion."

 **takeaway**

What are some areas in which God is calling you to the boldness of a lion?

reflect

_____

_____

_____

_____

_____

_____

_____

_____

_____

_____

_____

section 12
A SPIRIT OF EXCELLENCE

⏰ minute 57

A TWO-MILE CULTURE

Culture has been defined as the shared patterns of thought and behavior, relationships, and understanding that are learned through socialization. What would the world be like if religious people spent less time focusing on the debatable portions of Scripture and created a counterculture that practiced just a few of the teachings that are crystal clear? Let's experiment for a moment and ignore every statement Jesus made, except one: "If someone forces you to go one mile, go with him two miles" (Matthew 5:41).

IMAGINE WORKPLACES WHERE EVERYONE DOES MORE THAN REQUIRED.

Imagine workplaces where everyone does more than required. Imagine homes where every family member gives to the next more than they deserve. Imagine marriages where the most pressing question in the relationship is not, "How can I get more?" but "What more can I give?" Maybe I am a dreamer, but imagine what the world would be like if Christians really began to follow Christ.

takeaway

Identify ways in which you can pursue a "two-mile" culture in your life, work, or family.

reflect

_____

_____

_____

_____

_____

_____

_____

_____

_____

_____

_____

⏱ minute 58

BRING SIMPLE BACK

The key to healthy relationships is simple—love others as yourself. The key to weight loss is simple—move more and eat better. The key to creating wealth is equally simple—invest wisely and waste less. Life can be simple, but sometimes doing the right thing can be hard.

IF YOU PRAISE HIM WHILE IN DISTRESS, HE WILL RAISE YOU OUT OF THE TEST.

Paul says in Romans 7:21, "When I want to do good, evil is right there with me." He goes on to say, "Who will rescue me from this body of death?" (v. 24). In these verses, he was saying that sometimes his walk with God made him feel like he was buried with a corpse in a casket and he was slowly running out of air. This was a terribly painful situation. But Paul ends this crisis by saying, "Thanks be to God—through Jesus Christ our Lord" (v. 25).

In the midst of his trial, he released the solution and gave thanks and praise. If you praise Him while in distress, He will raise you out of the test. No matter how low you have *sunk*, if you begin to thank God in the middle of your *funk*, God will give you the grace to slam-*dunk* in the middle of all the *junk*.

 **takeaway**

What is a trial you are facing that you could respond to with praise, in spite of what you see?

reflect

_____

_____

_____

_____

_____

_____

_____

_____

_____

_____

⏱ minute 59

THE POWER OF FOCUS AND FORGETTING

Some time ago, I did some martial-arts training with one of my sons. When it came to breaking boards, I was a little intimidated. But the instructor trained us to mentally see our hands go to a point beyond the wood before we struck. We were to use all of our strength to move our hands to that point beyond the board. On my first try, I broke a board that I would never have imagined that I could break.

The apostle Paul understood the power of focus. In Philippians 3:13-14, he said, "But one thing I do: Forgetting what is behind and straining toward what is ahead, I press on toward the goal to win the prize."

Focus and forgetting are two sides of the same coin. To focus, we have to filter out the extraneous and zoom in to the vital. Who we used to be becomes irrelevant if we get a big enough vision of who God is making us. This journey really begins in the heart. We have to see ourselves where we want to be, before we are ready to go.

 **takeaway**

What is a distraction that frequently hinders your ability to focus and therefore get where you need to go?

reflect

_____

_____

_____

_____

_____

_____

_____

_____

_____

_____

_____

⏲ minute 60

EXCELLENCE

Actor Michael J. Fox made this statement: "I am careful not to confuse excellence with perfection. Excellence, I can reach for; perfection is God's business."[14] The most anyone can ever do in life is his or her very best. Sometimes we find that our best is not enough, and in such moments all that we can do is trust God.

ALL OF US MUST MAKE PEACE WITH THE FACT THAT WE ARE LESS THAN PERFECT.

The King James Version of the Bible says in Psalm 138:8, "The Lord will perfect that which concerneth me." I do not know what Michael J. Fox believes about God, but he stated a biblical truth. All of us must make peace with the fact that we are less than perfect. But we must daily wage war against any notion that we should settle for being anything less than excellent.

takeaway

What is an area of your life that, although you will not perfect, you can increase in excellence?

reflect

_____

_____

_____

_____

_____

_____

_____

_____

_____

_____

_____

_____

section 13
PERSONAL GROWTH

⊕ minute 61

DISCOVERING GOD'S WILL FOR YOUR LIFE

First Thessalonians 5:16–18 says, "Rejoice always, pray continually, give thanks in all circumstances; for this is God's will for you." If you are wondering what God's will is for your life, question no more.

DISCOVERING GOD'S WILL FOR OUR LIVES BEGINS WITH AN ATTITUDE, NOT AN ASSIGNMENT.

God's will is that we rejoice, pray, and be thankful, no matter our circumstances. You might say, "How could God ask for so much from us?" I say, "Why did He ask us for so little?" Even if we don't have a lot to be thankful for in life, we can be thankful for this: When we are good, God loves us. When we are bad, He loves us. When we are confused, He loves us. When we are sad, He loves us.

If you did not think you had anything to be thankful for a few minutes ago, you should now. Discovering God's will for our lives begins with an attitude, not an assignment. Take a few minutes to personally experience God's will by being grateful.

 **takeaway**

What are some of the negative circumstances that you have faced for which you can now be grateful as you look at His grace through them?

reflect

_____

_____

_____

_____

_____

_____

_____

_____

_____

_____

_____

⏲ minute 62

IMITATION

To be a disciple of Christ is a powerful thing. Discipleship not only implies submission but also imitation. Jesus said in Matthew 10:25, "It is enough for students to be *like* their teachers, and servants *like* their masters." Genuine discipleship causes imitation.

No matter how loudly you sing or how often you attend church on Sunday, if you act like the Devil the rest of the week, you are not a disciple of Christ. Genuine disciples have bad days, make bad choices, and even sin, but this is the exception and not the rule.

GENUINE DISCIPLESHIP CAUSES IMITATION.

We miss the mark for one of three reasons.

1. We try to live up to the wrong standards. (We follow human ideas instead of God's Word.)

2. We have the wrong source of strength. (We try to do it by sheer willpower instead of reliance on the Holy Spirit.)

3. We have the wrong motives. (We are trying to please people and not God.)

To love Jesus is to ask Him to help you be like Him.

 **takeaway**

Identify some of the standards, sources of strength and motives that drive your discipleship.

reflect

_____

_____

_____

_____

_____

_____

_____

_____

_____

_____

_____

_____

_____

⏱ minute 63

STOP COPING

I heard someone say today that COPE stands for Covering, Over, Pain, Effectively. In church, people can become masters at coping, experts at masking the pain in their hearts. We learn to get our praise *on* and lift our hands *up*. We give the person sitting *beside* us a high five, and after church, we know how to go to our favorite restaurants and *get down*. But Jesus did not die for us to create a new *coping* mechanism. He rose to give us a new *hoping* mechanism.

GOD WILL BE MORE REAL TO YOU, WHEN YOU GET REAL WITH HIM.

When is the last time you really told the Lord what was going on in your heart? David said in Psalm 18:6 (ESV), "In my distress I called upon the Lord." David did not pretend that he was okay when he was not. He said, "To my God I cried for help. From his temple he heard my voice, and my cry to him reached his ears." God will be more real to you, when you get real with Him. Do more than *cope*. Begin to put your full *hope* in God's compassion and desire to help.

takeaway

What are some of the areas of
your life that you gravitate toward
coping mechanisms versus "realness"
with God?

reflect

_____

_____

_____

_____

_____

_____

_____

_____

_____

_____

HOW FAR WE HAVE COME

Ephesians 4:15 says, "Speaking the truth in love, we will grow." Did you know that God does not require us to be perfect, but He does expect us to grow? Paul finished the verse by saying, "to become in every respect the mature body." God wants us not only to grow but also to mature.

THE REAL MEASUREMENT OF PROGRESS IS NOT HOW PERFECT WE ARE, BUT HOW FAR WE HAVE COME.

When my kids were in diapers, I did not enjoy changing them, but I never got mad at them for making it so I had to. My kids did what healthy children did at that stage of life.

God has often had to clean up after me. Instead of being angry, God understood that it was just a stage of life, and I would soon get past it. God is not requiring that any of us come to Him behaving perfectly, but He does desire that we improve. The real measurement of progress is not how perfect we are, but how far we have come.

 **takeaway**

As you look at your life, what are some of the areas in which you have made noticeable progress and growth?

reflect

_____

_____

_____

_____

_____

_____

_____

_____

_____

_____

_____

_____

EXTRAORDINARY

I heard someone say that only five letters stand between ordinary and extraordinary: e–x–t–r–a. Investing just a little extra effort, a little extra focus, and just a little extra time can make a remarkable difference in your life.

OFTEN IT'S NOT THE BIG THINGS THAT GET IN THE WAY OF PROGRESS BUT THE LITTLE THINGS.

Song of Solomon 2:15 explains that it is the little foxes that ruin the vine. Often it's not the big things that get in the way of life and progress; it's the little things.

When I wanted to lose weight, cutting out sodas for a month and drinking a little extra water helped me lose pounds. When our budget became tight, a little more staying-in versus going-out saved us hundreds of dollars each month. Our family started to get a little disconnected, so we simply decided to turn off the TV while eating dinner. A little extra conversation turned our house back into a home. It only takes a little *extra* to start living an extraordinary life.

 **takeaway**

What are several areas of incremental change that would yield great dividends in your life if applied consistently?

reflect

_____

_____

_____

_____

_____

_____

_____

_____

_____

_____

_____

⏱ minute 66

HANDLING RESPONSIBILITY

The early church not only experienced explosive growth but also explosive problems. In Acts 6:3, the apostles came up with the solution. "Brothers and sisters, choose seven men from among you who are known to be full of the Spirit and wisdom. We will turn this responsibility over to them." There are dozens of leadership principles in this one verse, but during a very challenging period, the one word that jumped off the page was *responsibility*.

THE WAY THE DISCIPLES HANDLED THEIR GROWING RESPONSIBILITIES WAS TO GIVE THEM AWAY.

The word can be broken into two parts: *response* and *ability*. It became clear that if God gave me responsibility, it is because He has placed in me the ability to respond appropriately to the given demands. Accepting responsibility does not mean that we must do everything ourselves. The way the disciples handled their growing responsibilities was to give them away. The best leaders do not measure themselves by what they can do themselves but by what they can do through others.

 **takeaway**

What are several responsibilities that you could appropriately "give away," freeing you up to do what you can do best?

reflect

_____

_____

_____

_____

_____

_____

_____

_____

_____

_____

⏱ minute 67

GIVING

Ralph Waldo Emerson observed, "One of the most beautiful compensations of this life is that we cannot sincerely try to help others without helping ourselves."[15] In Luke 6:38, Jesus put it this way, "Give, and it will be given to you."

GIVING ALWAYS DOES MORE FOR THE GIVER THAN THE RECEIVER.

The very act of giving frees us from the burden of only having ourselves on our minds. Giving always does more for the giver than the receiver. Giving is the highest expression of God's image in us. Generosity is not an obligation but a privilege. Look for an opportunity to help you by helping someone else today. Remember to do it with no strings attached if you want to experience the greatest benefits of giving.

takeaway

Identify someone you could help "with no strings attached" and thereby receive the benefits of giving.

reflect

_____

_____

_____

_____

_____

_____

_____

_____

_____

_____

_____

KNOW WHEN TO RUN

There is an old country song that I found to be very instructive when dealing with temptation. "You got to know when to hold 'em, know when to fold 'em. Know when to walk away, know when to run."[16]

WHEN YOUR PERSONAL RESISTANCE FAILS, DON'T BE ABOVE PUTTING ON YOUR RUNNING SHOES.

Genesis 39:6–12 says,

> Now Joseph was well-built and handsome, and after a while his master's wife took notice of Joseph and said, "Come to bed with me!" But he refused ... Then, one day, Joseph went into the house to attend to his duties, and none of the household servants were inside. She caught him by his cloak and said, "Come to bed with me!" But he left his cloak in her hand and ran out of the house.

Joseph did more than attempt to resist; he knew when it was time to run. When your personal resistance fails, don't be above putting on your running shoes. Learning when to resist, and when to leave the room, may determine whose bed you wind up in tonight.

 **takeaway**

How do you typically respond to temptation, and what would it take for you to "know when to run"?

reflect

_____

_____

_____

_____

_____

_____

_____

_____

_____

_____

_____

HOLD YOUR HORSES

Abraham was the first to call God "Jehovah Jireh," which some say literally means, "the One who sees ahead and provides." The name encapsulates the fact that whatever God calls for, He will first provide for.

Imagine if God created Adam on the first day. Since the ground was not made until the third day, Adam would have had to swim forty-eight hours before he could stand. If Adam had to wait his turn, then so will you and I.

WHATEVER GOD CALLS FOR, HE WILL FIRST PROVIDE FOR.

Ecclesiastes 3:11 says, "He has made everything beautiful in its time." Like the movement in a well-oiled engine, keeping pace with God is a beautiful thing.

When we lag behind or get ahead of God's timing, what was intended for glory becomes another story. What He intended to bless can quickly turn into a mess. The problem is never God's unfaithfulness, but sometimes our impatience. Hold your horses, and you will one day hold your blessings.

 **takeaway**

When was a time you got ahead of God's timing and forfeited a greater blessing due to your impatience?

reflect

_____

_____

_____

_____

_____

_____

_____

_____

_____

_____

_____

_____

⏱ minute 70

A JOYFUL HEART

Proverbs 17:22 says, "A joyful heart is good medicine." (ESV) Before modern science acknowledged the connectivity between our bodies and souls, the writer of Proverbs was inspired to observe that cheerfulness does a body good. Our disposition of mind has a profound impact upon the condition of our bodies. Proverbs continues, "But a crushed spirit dries up the bones." A sorrowful heart not only weakens our nerves but also impacts our very bones. The writer is teaching us that no emotion has a greater capacity for destruction than unresolved bitterness and grief.

A SORROWFUL HEART NOT ONLY WEAKENS OUR NERVES BUT ALSO IMPACTS OUR VERY BONES.

Sometimes, we should look deeper at our physical symptoms; they may be trying to point at more profound issues. If we learn to lighten up and brighten up, we may all make fewer trips to the doctor. Life is too short to live it sad.

 **takeaway**

Are there any physical issues you face that may have spiritual roots?

reflect

_____

_____

_____

_____

_____

_____

_____

_____

_____

_____

_____

_____

_____

⏱ minute 71

BACK IN THE DRIVER'S SEAT

One thing I love about Jesus is how deliberate He is. When speaking of his impending death, He flipped the script and said, "No man takes my life but I lay it down." When Peter took issue with Him saying He would die on the cross, Jesus refused to let a human relationship get in the way of his relationship with His heavenly Father, and He sternly rebuked the senior disciple. Then Jesus made this telling statement in John 15:16 to all his disciples: "You did not choose me, but I chose you." Jesus made choices about who was in His life and did not leave such decisions to circumstances or others.

YOU CANNOT CHANGE YOUR PAST, BUT YOU CAN CHANGE YOUR FUTURE.

Life is too short to let other people live it for you. It is important that you start sitting in the driver's seat of your life. You cannot change your past, but you can change your future. Start by making prayerful choices about who is in it.

takeaway

Is there anyone (or anything) that has an inordinate influence on your life, removing you from the driver's seat?

reflect

_____

_____

_____

_____

_____

_____

_____

_____

_____

_____

_____

_____

⏰ minute 72

A STICK FOR BACKS OF FOOLS

Proverbs 26:3 says, "A whip for the horse, a halter for the donkey, and a rod for the back of fools!" Why is a stick destined for the backs of fools? Because if we are not responsive when God speaks to us through His Word and as the voice of our consciences, God has to speak to us through the only language a fool understands: pain.

SOMETIMES OUR LIVES ARE HARD BECAUSE OUR HEADS ARE SO HARD.

We sometimes hurt in our lives, not because God does not love us but because we would not listen any other way. When my children were little, I would say, "If you do not listen to my mouth, you will have to feel my hand." This is frowned upon today, but it worked well for my kids. They became fast learners.

If we have a soft heart before God, He can deal with us gently. But if our hearts are hard, we force God to be hard. Sometimes our lives are hard because our heads are so hard.

 **takeaway**

In what areas are you facing discomfort that may actually be God's discipline as he attempts to get your attention?

reflect

_____

_____

_____

_____

_____

_____

_____

_____

_____

_____

TIPS FOR CONFRONTATION

Confrontation contains the prefix *con*, which means "together," and the root *fron*, which means "face." It speaks of the act of coming together face-to-face to resolve an issue. Confrontation is a normal part of life and a skill that you must master if you want to be successful.

Two questions may help you in this area. Before your next confrontation, ask yourself, "Should I confront this person or let it go?" Proverbs 19:11 says, "It is to one's glory to overlook an offense." In other words, do not be petty. Be big enough to let the minor slights and digs pass, and only confront when you need to.

Secondly, ask yourself if your attitude is right. A confrontation with a friend should never be about retaliation. Avoid attacking the person's motivations and character. Only God knows what is really going on in a person's heart. Focus only on the behavior and the impact that the person's behavior has on him or her and you in particular. An old saying will help you maintain your boundaries in the midst of conflict: "Keep your words sweet, because you may have to eat them."

 **takeaway**

What is a situation you should confront with biblical truth?

reflect

_____

_____

_____

_____

_____

_____

_____

_____

_____

_____

_____

_____

_____

⏰ minute 74

MAKING THE MOST OF MY TIME

Today, I want to borrow some insights from John Maxwell. He stated, "We cannot manage time. We can only manage opportunities."[17] We cannot change how much time we are given, but we can take advantage of each day's opportunities. Time is life's most precious commodity. He goes on to say, "We cannot change time, only our priorities."[18] Everyone gets twenty-four hours in a day, but how we use our time is what makes the difference.

Wise people do not spend time but invest it. What we value in life is seen clearest by how we make use of our time. Why do we spend so much time watching other people live on television, instead of living ourselves? Real life has no reruns. Why do we spend so much time trying to impress people we do not really know and, if we are honest, do not even like? Many of the people who are so important to us today will probably not even be in our lives five years from now. People, places, and things will change, but we will never get any more time than the time we have spent. So invest it in the things that really matter.

takeaway

Identify several areas of your life in which you spend rather than invest in things that matter.

reflect

_____

_____

_____

_____

_____

_____

_____

_____

_____

_____

_____

_____

⏱ minute 75

NO MORE MONKEY BUSINESS

I have heard that in Australia there is a special method for catching monkeys. People put a piece of fruit in a little box with a hole big enough for the monkey to stick his open hand through. The hunters then leave the boxes under a tree overnight and return in the morning to find the monkeys with their hands caught and unable to get free.

OUR INABILITY TO LET GO OF THE THINGS THAT ARE IN OUR POSSESSION IS OFTEN THE REASON WHY WE ARE TRAPPED.

The box would release an open hand but not a fist. All the monkeys had to do to get out of the trap was to open their hands. But once the monkey had the piece of fruit in hand, he refused to let go of it.

Our inability to let go of the things that are in our possession is often the reason why we stay trapped longer than we should.

 **takeaway**

What are the things you need to release to make progress in your personal, spiritual or professional life?

reflect

_____

_____

_____

_____

_____

_____

_____

_____

_____

_____

_____

_____

⏰ minute 76

BREAKING HABITS

A habit is anything we do repetitively without consciously thinking about it. The brain is a sophisticated and efficient machine. It is prewired not waste its time starting from scratch every time a decision needs to be made. Our brains are designed take what we have done in the past as our recommendation of what we want to do in the future.

If our past decisions were good, this pre-wiring will serve us well. But if our past decisions were poor, we can easily become trapped by our past behavior.

Romans 12:2 says, "Do not conform to the pattern of this world, but be transformed by the renewing of your mind." The best way to overcome an old behavior is by creating a new one. Give your mind better recommendations to choose from. Your mind was designed to be influenced by your behavior. Your old habits begin with a choice, and new ones can begin with a choice. I am not promising that it will be easy, but I am saying that the choice is yours.

 **takeaway**

Identify several repetitive and unconscious habits that you have developed, as well as accompanying new positive habits that you can cultivate?

reflect

_____

_____

_____

_____

_____

_____

_____

_____

_____

_____

⏱ minute 77

RENEWED REASONING

Hebrews 11:17–19 says, "By faith Abraham, when God tested him, offered Isaac as a sacrifice, even though God had said to him, 'It is through Isaac that your offspring will be reckoned.' Listen to the next verse. "Abraham reasoned that God could even raise the dead." Don't miss this. Abraham did not have a specific word from God that his son would come back to life; he simply surmised it.

Sometimes we do not need God to speak as much as God needs us to learn how to think.

Many of us are waiting on a word from God to calm our fears. But when we begin to reason properly, many of our apprehensions will go away by themselves. "Abraham *reasoned* that God could even raise the dead" (emphasis added). How do you think when you are in crisis? Do you reason like Father Abraham? "If God led me here, He must have a plan to get me out." Or "If this difficult thing happened, I must have the wherewithal to handle it, because God promised that we would not be tempted beyond what we can bear."

Our lives will never rise higher than our level of thought.

takeaway

In what ways does your thinking need to be renewed to better align with God's will?

reflect

_____

_____

_____

_____

_____

_____

_____

_____

_____

_____

_____

_____

⏱ minute 78

TRUST

Sometimes people get confused over the difference love and trust. Scripture teaches us to love unconditionally but never tells us to trust unconditionally. Jesus says in Luke 16:10, "Whoever can be trusted with very little can also be trusted with much, and whoever is dishonest with very little will also be dishonest with much." The principle is that before we trust people with big things, we need to give them a chance to prove themselves with small things.

BEFORE WE TRUST PEOPLE WITH BIG THINGS, WE NEED TO GIVE THEM A CHANCE TO PROVE THEMSELVES WITH SMALL THINGS.

Proverbs 11:22 says, "Like a gold ring in a pig's snout is a beautiful woman who shows no discretion." Discretion is the restraint people who realize their significance must use, to protect their lives from abuse. If we make our most valued treasures free for the asking, Scripture says it is like putting a five-karat nose ring in the snout of a pig. The pig does not know the ring's value and will only take what is precious to you back into its mud.

Love everyone, but let people earn your trust. If you do this, you will be able to spend less time in the mud.

 **takeaway**

Think of a time in which you entrusted an untrustworthy person with something they didn't value.

reflect

_____

_____

_____

_____

_____

_____

_____

_____

_____

_____

_____

_____

⏱ minute 79

MUCH FRUIT

Jesus says in John 15:8 (ESV), "By this My Father is glorified, that you bear much fruit." How long would an owner of an orchard keep trees that were just hanging on, barely surviving and not producing fruit? Not long. The owner would eventually cut those trees down and plant new ones. The farmer did not plant the trees for them to merely exist. They were planted to produce.

THE PROOF OF OUR DISCIPLESHIP IS NOT ONLY OUR CHURCH ATTENDANCE OR THE SONGS WE SING BUT ALSO THE LIVES WE LIVE.

Jesus said, "By this my Father is glorified, that you bear much fruit and so prove to be my disciples." As the orchard owner does not plant trees just to take up space but to produce, so does our heavenly Father create us with an expectation of fruitfulness. The proof of our discipleship is not only our church attendance or the songs we sing but also the lives we live. God has not designed us just to be present; He has created us to thrive.

 **takeaway**

What are some of the areas of fruitfulness in your life—as well as areas that need more cultivation?

reflect

_____

_____

_____

_____

_____

_____

_____

_____

_____

_____

_____

⏲ minute 80

MAKING A CONSEQUENCE

We are free to choose, but we will never be free from the consequences of our choices. God said to Adam and Eve in Genesis 2:17, "You must not eat from the tree of the knowledge of good and evil, for when you eat of it you will certainly die." God gave Adam and Eve the liberty to choose or reject Him at the tree, but He also made clear that they would have to live with the consequences of their choice.

MAKING A DECISION IS NOT HARD; IT IS LIVING WITH THE CONSEQUENCES OF OUR DECISIONS THAT CAN BE TOUGH.

Making a decision is not hard; it is living with the consequences of our decisions that's tough. Always keep in mind that every time you make a decision, your decision is also making a consequence. If you can't live with the consequence, don't make the decision.

 **takeaway**

How have you seen—in retrospect—
negative consequences in your life for
decisions that were easy to make?

reflect

_____

_____

_____

_____

_____

_____

_____

_____

_____

_____

_____

_____

THE FIRST STEP

When I was a little kid, I used to sit in my friend's old car and pretend to drive. When the car was in neutral but not moving, it was almost impossible to turn the wheel. We cannot change the direction of a car unless it is in motion. Likewise, God cannot steer the lives of people who insist on sitting still.

IF YOU ARE NOT WILLING TO TAKE YOUR FIRST STEP, YOU WILL NOT HEAR GOD'S NEXT STEP.

You might say, "When God gives me a complete plan, then I will move." But Psalm 37:23 (KJV) says, "The *steps* of a good man are ordered by the LORD" (emphasis added). If you are not willing to take your first step, you will not hear God's next step. God often shows us His plan, one step at a time. A little motion in the direction you think you need to go may turn your life around.

 **takeaway**

Identify opportunities for which you are awaiting guidance from God and for which you could take a first step?

reflect

_____

_____

_____

_____

_____

_____

_____

_____

_____

_____

_____

_____

⏲ minute 82

WHAT WE BELIEVE ABOUT OURSELVES

Carter G. Woodson said,

> If you can control a man's thinking, you don't have to worry about his actions. If you can determine what a man thinks you don't have to worry about what he will do. If you can make a man feel he is inferior, you don't have to compel him to seek inferior status, he will do so without being told and if you can make a man believe that he is justly an outcast, you don't have to order him to the backdoor, he will go to the backdoor on his own and if there is no backdoor, the very nature of the man will demand that he build one.[19]

We will always act in a manner consistent with what we believe about ourselves. Proverbs 23:7 (KJV) says, "As a man thinks in his heart so is he." Change your mind, and you will change your life.

takeaway

How have your thought patterns regarding your perceived inferiority in certain areas limited your ability to change?

reflect

_____

_____

_____

_____

_____

_____

_____

_____

_____

_____

WHEN WILL MY MAN BE READY?

Marriage is not for everyone. Jesus was single. Paul, Daniel, John the Baptist, and many others lived powerful lives without being married. But for those women who want to marry, how do you know when a man is ready for marriage?

Three things were present in Adam before God brought Eve.

1. The man had a job. Genesis 2:15 says, "The LORD God took the man and put him in the Garden of Eden to work it and take care of it." Ladies, your attitude should be, "No money, no honey."

2. Adam knew God's voice. Verse 16 says, "And the Lord God commanded the man, 'You are free to eat from any tree in the garden.'" Ladies, your attitude should be, "Don't know God, won't know me."

3. Adam had clear boundaries in his life. In verse 17, the Lord said to Adam, "You must not eat from the tree of the knowledge of good and evil, for when you eat from it you will certainly die." Ladies, if a man can't tell himself "no," you'd better.

 **takeaway**

How would you apply the concepts of marriage readiness to your own situation—married or single?

reflect

_____

_____

_____

_____

_____

_____

_____

_____

_____

_____

_____

_____

⏱ minute 84

HOW TO OVERCOME TEMPER

I have not taken a taken a DNA test, but I have a very diverse ethnicity. Both of my parents are African American, but my middle name is "McCurry" as I am the namesake of my great grandfather who was Irish. Therefore, I can easily fit both the stereotypes of an angry Black man and the Irish temper. On top of this, my father's father was a full-blooded Native American, so you can imagine how I might react to watching movies like *Amistad, Braveheart,* and *Dances with Wolves.*

Kidding aside, I really do understand what it means to have a temper. The thing that helped me manage my temper was first understanding that anger is not bad in itself. Even Jesus got angry and turned over tables. Ephesians 4:26 does not say, "In your anger, you sin," but "In your anger, *do* not sin."

When righteousness is violated, it is healthy to feel angry. How we handle this emotion is key. When I feel angry, I have learned to try to attack the problem and not the person. I try to focus on the principles involved more than the personalities. I am not always as successful at this as I would like, but I am getting better.

 **takeaway**

How do you identify the difference between sinful anger and anger that is not sinful (according to Ephesians 4:26 in your own life?

reflect

_____

_____

_____

_____

_____

_____

_____

_____

_____

_____

⏲ minute 85

HOW NOT TO HANDLE MISTAKES

There are three things we should not to do when we make a mistake.

1. Don't try to cover it up.
2. Don't try to cover it up.
3. Don't try to cover it up.

In politics, people say the cover-up is always worse than the crime. Our instinct for self-preservation can get us into a lot of trouble. When David tried to cover up his sin with Bathsheba, sex evolved into deception and then into murder. David could have recovered from his initial sin, but he never recovered from the attempted cover-up.

Here are three steps that can help you when you miss:

1. Admit your mistake quickly. Don't delay the inevitable.
2. Accept responsibility. The Devil did not make you do it, though he probably helped you out. You did it.
3. Ask for help from someone who is qualified to help. Authority should not be run from but run to, when we are in trouble.

 **takeaway**

Recall a time when you attempted to cover up a mistake—as well as the consequences that you faced as a result.

reflect

_____

_____

_____

_____

_____

_____

_____

_____

_____

_____

_____

section 14
RELATIONSHIPS

SELF-RESPECT

Are things in life happening to you or are you making your life happen? In Deuteronomy 28:13, Moses said, "The Lord will make you the head and not the tail." What is the difference between being a head and a tail? First, the view is much better. But secondly, the head makes decisions that the tail is obligated to follow.

IT'S AMAZING HOW PEOPLE WILL RESPECT A PERSON WHO DECIDES TO RESPECT THEMSELVES.

I remember the day I got tired of my own victimization. People were pushing, pulling, and grabbing at me to make me what they wanted me to be, until I recognized that it is impossible to please everyone.

I realized that no matter what I did, I would face criticism and certain people would find fault with me. I decided that, if I was going to be talked about anyway, I might as well be talked about for being myself. I decided I would no longer suffer for trying to be the person it seemed everyone else wanted me to be and I could never be. But I would be willing to take the heat for being the person I really am. It's amazing how people will respect a person who decides to respect themselves.

 **takeaway**

Recall a time when your lack of self-respect led to a lack of respect from others?

reflect

_____

_____

_____

_____

_____

_____

_____

_____

_____

_____

_____

_____

⏱ minute 87

SAYING "NO" WITHOUT EXPLANATION

When Nehemiah's enemies discovered that he had rebuilt the wall and filled in the gaps, they sent him this message: "Come, let us meet together in one of the villages on the plain of Ono." (Nehemiah 6:3–4) But Nehemiah discerned that it was a trap. So he replied, "I am carrying on a great project and cannot go down. Four times they sent me the same message, and each time I gave them the same answer."

GOD IS LOVE, BUT GOD IS ALSO WISE.

I can think of dozens of times that I knew in my gut that I was being set up, but in my attempt to be nice, I took the meeting anyway. I have regretted it every time. Scripture says God is love, but it also teaches us that God is wise. I have learned that I do not have to answer every call or accept every invitation. Scripture teaches that we are to owe no man anything but love. It requires me to be kind to everyone, but as an older man once said to me, "A sign of maturity is sometimes being able to say 'no' without explanation."

takeaway

Do you struggle with always having to give an reason for saying "no"? If so, why is that the case?

reflect

_____

_____

_____

_____

_____

_____

_____

_____

_____

_____

_____

⏱ minute 88

HOW WE STAYED MARRIED

I was at a conference recently and said to myself, "If I hear another 'ought to' message without the speaker explaining to me 'how to,' my head is going to explode. We all know we ought to be better; the question is 'How?'"

WHEN OUR PRIMARY GOAL WAS TO GIVE LOVE AND NOT GET LOVE, OUR RELATIONSHIP TOOK OFF.

Young men often ask me, "How have you remained faithful to your wife?" Based on today's headlines, it is certainly not because I am a preacher. My wife and I have had our challenges, but marriage for us was not just about getting our respective needs met. We took seriously the biblical admonition, "Take up your cross and follow me." (Matthew 16:24, ESV) Sometimes, I was her beam, and sometimes, she was mine.

My goal as a husband is not to have someone who loves me, though my wife does more than I deserve. My goal is to find ways to love my wife. When our primary goal was to give love and not get love, our relationship took off. Marriage is one of the greatest opportunities in life to help people get over themselves.

 **takeaway**

How has your marriage or relationships in your life helped you "get over yourself"?

reflect

_____

_____

_____

_____

_____

_____

_____

_____

_____

_____

_____

_____

LOVE GOD, LOVE PEOPLE AND MOVE ON

Romans 12:20–21 says, "If your enemy is hungry, feed him; if he is thirsty, give him something to drink. In doing this, you will heap burning coals on his head. Do not be overcome by evil, but overcome evil with good."

OUR BITTERNESS SAYS MORE ABOUT US THAN THOSE WHO HAVE DONE US WRONG.

If you want to have an effective walk with God, you must keep in mind that God cares about our enemies as much as He cares for us. We often have great excuses for why we have soured in our walk with God, but it usually can be narrowed down to one thing: love. At some point, we stop forgiving people. We have to remember that our bitterness says more about us than those who have done us wrong. Forgiveness is my gift to others, but moving on is my gift to myself.

 **takeaway**

Recall a time when, instead of returning evil or becoming bitter over an offense, you forgave.

reflect

_____

_____

_____

_____

_____

_____

_____

_____

_____

_____

⏰ minute 90

CRAZY PEOPLE

Galatians 3:2–6 from The Message Bible says,

> Let me put this question to you: How did your new life begin? Was it by working your heads off to please God? Or was it by responding to God's Message to you? ... Only crazy people would think they could complete by their own efforts what was begun by God. If you weren't smart enough or strong enough to begin it, how do you suppose you could perfect it? ... Answer this question: Does the God who lavishly provides you with his own presence, his Holy Spirit, working things in your lives you could never do for yourselves, does he do these things because of your strenuous moral striving or because you trust him to do them in you? Don't these things happen among you just as they happened with Abraham? He believed God, and that act of belief was turned into a life that was right with God.

Paul is saying that when we learn to trust God, we no longer have to try so hard.

 **takeaway**

Do you struggle to earn God's approval through your own effort? Reflect on the truth of Galatians 3 and its truth in your life.

reflect

_____

_____

_____

_____

_____

_____

_____

_____

_____

_____

⏱ minute 91

COMING OUT OF YOUR SHELL

Because of my public life, people are surprised to find that I am not naturally an extrovert but an introvert. I have spent most of my early life somewhat withdrawn. I still do not enjoy being the center of attention, but there is a night-and-day difference between my disposition a few years ago and my attitude today. What happened? What helped me grow?

I discovered at the core of every insecurity is typically selfishness or ignorance. Selfishness, because people cannot be insecure without having themselves on their minds; ignorance, because Psalm 139:14 removes the foundation for all personal insecurity by declaring, "I am fearfully and wonderfully made." *Fearfully* literally means "awe-inspiring." *Wonderfully* communicates the idea of being in a class by oneself. According to Scripture, I am awesome and in a class by myself.

If I believed what this psalm said about me, it would be selfish of me to keep me only to myself. The first step to coming out of a shell is realizing that you are valuable and have something of value to offer to others.

 **takeaway**

What are the parts of you that are particularly "awe-inspiring"—those God made to add value to others?

reflect

_____

_____

_____

_____

_____

_____

_____

_____

_____

_____

_____

⏱ minute 92

CHECK THE GARBAGE AT THE DOOR

A good team requires both strong coaching and honest communication. When Jesus built his team, He created a culture of openness and honesty within the team. Matthew 16:22–23 is one such example.

Jesus had been talking about his impending death and "Peter took Jesus aside and began to rebuke him. Saying, 'Never, Lord! This shall never happen to you.'" On a good team, the team members are free to speak their minds. But watch this: Jesus turned to Peter and said, "Get behind me, Satan. You are a stumbling block to me. You do not have the concerns of God but merely human concerns."

On a healthy team, not only can the players speak frankly, but so can the coach. I invite my staff to be open and honest with me, but under one condition—I can be equally frank. I have no problem with people telling me about myself, as long as they recognize it is a two-way street, and they are comfortable with me doing the same to them.

 **takeaway**

Do you welcome others to speak into your life—even when it's something you may not want to hear?

💬 **reflect**

_____

_____

_____

_____

_____

_____

_____

_____

_____

_____

_____

⏰ minute 93

YOU GET WHAT YOU CHOOSE

In Joshua 24:15, God said, "Choose for yourselves today whom you will serve." We do not get what we want in life; we get what we choose. We cannot control everything that happens to us, but we can control our responses.

AS MUCH AS HE LOVES US, HE CANNOT MAKE OUR CHOICES FOR US.

God can do anything, but one thing He will not do is choose for us. As much as He loves us, He cannot make our choices for us. The best marital advice I ever gave is this: Your central concern in your marriage is not how your spouse treats you, but how you treat your spouse. God never measures us based on how others treat us but on how we treat others.

takeaway

If "God measures us on how we treat others," how do you measure up?

reflect

_____

_____

_____

_____

_____

_____

_____

_____

_____

_____

_____

_____

⏰ minute 94

ASK FOR HELP

Mark 15:20–21 says, "And when they had mocked him ... Then they led him out to crucify him." It was customary for the condemned to carry their own cross, but after the events of the last fifteen hours:

- the agonies of Gethsemane, including sweating drops of blood;

- the betrayal of Judas;

- the desertion of His own disciples;

- the denial of His leading disciple, Peter;

- the bloody beating with a Roman nine-prong whip; and

- the crown of thorns and several beatings by the soldiers.

Tradition says Jesus fell under the weight of the cross. The most powerful man who had ever lived became too weak to carry His own load. The Bible says a man from Cyrene was passing by and the soldiers forced him to carry the cross. If Jesus stumbled under the weight of his cross, don't be surprised if you will at times. Just be humble enough to accept help.

takeaway

Recall a time in which you resisted taking help from someone—and the results of your resistance.

reflect

_____

_____

_____

_____

_____

_____

_____

_____

_____

_____

_____

_____

⏱ minute 95

STRONG MARRIAGE

I know you have heard me say this before, but I am going to keep saying this until it registers. After years of mentoring couples, I think that the best marriage counseling that could be offered to a starry-eyed couple is to hand them three nails, a hammer, and a cross and tell them they are going to need it.

MARRIAGE IS GOD'S SENSE OF HUMOR.

We have no idea how self-centered we are until we choose to live and make decisions with another person in sickness and health, till death do we part. Marriage is God's sense of humor having a head-on collision with our self-importance.

Galatians 5:24 says, "Those who belong to Christ Jesus have crucified the flesh with its passions and desires." It did not say that those who go to church have crucified the flesh but those who "belong to Christ." It requires more than attending church to stay in relationships; it takes holiness. Holiness has nothing to do with alcohol, tobacco, or the length of your dress. True holiness is about the holes in your hands and feet. Two truly *hole-y* people will find a way to work it out and stay together.

 **takeaway**

What are some of the ways your marriage or relationships have helped make you holy?

reflect

_____

_____

_____

_____

_____

_____

_____

_____

_____

_____

_____

⏱ minute 96

STAR

Proverbs 11:14 says, "For lack of guidance a nation falls, but victory is won through many advisers." Since victory is won through many advisers, our success is not dependent on only what we know but who we listen to.

I have learned to use the STAR acronym to qualify my advisors.

- ="S" – Is the person **successful** in the area they offer advice? It is one thing to have an opinion, but it is far better to have a track record.

- ="T" – Will the person be **transparent** with me? I need to hear not only about successes but also failures, to truly learn what to avoid.

- ="A" – I don't have to always **agree** with the person. If I agree with everything that is said, I am probably not learning anything new.

- ="R" – I must **respect** the person. Respect is the currency of all true relationships.

If you soar with stars, you will eventually shine like one.

takeaway

Who are the STARs in your life, who provide you the guidance that helps you soar? If you don't have any, make a prospective list.

reflect

_____

_____

_____

_____

_____

_____

_____

_____

_____

_____

CHOOSE YOUR FRIENDS WISELY

In Mark 2:1–5, because a crowd had filled the house to hear Jesus, a paralyzed man could not get inside to meet Him. So his friends dug through the roof and lowered the paralyzed man on a mat. The Bible says Jesus saw their faith and healed him.

SOMETIMES, WE CAN'T GET BY WITHOUT A LITTLE HELP FROM OUR FRIENDS.

If the paralyzed man's friends were like many of our friends, they would have tried to talk him out of trying to get to Jesus. After all, Jesus was an important person, the house was too small, the crowd was too large, and the list goes on. But instead of discouraging the man, they carried him. Sometimes, we can't get by without a little help from our friends. The people we make our friends can make the difference between living outside the place of blessing and going through the roof.

 **takeaway**

Who are some friends who have helped you "through the roof" in a time of crisis—and who is someone for whom you have done the same?

reflect

_____

_____

_____

_____

_____

_____

_____

_____

_____

_____

⏰ minute 98

A FEW

One night, I was considering the state of our world and I cried out to the Lord, "Where is your honor? Where is your respect? Where is the fear of God in our nation?" After a few moments of silence, the Lord responded, "Where is your faith?"

GOD INTERVENING IN OUR WORLD IS NOT DEPENDENT ON THE WICKEDNESS OF THE WICKED BUT ON THE RIGHTEOUSNESS OF THE RIGHTEOUS.

In Genesis 18:23–26, Abraham argued with the Lord, "Will you sweep away the righteous with the wicked? What if there are fifty righteous people in the city. Will you really sweep it away and not spare the place for the sake of the fifty righteous people in it?" The Lord responded, "If I find fifty righteous people in the city of Sodom, I will spare the whole place for their sake." Then Abraham negotiated down to ten. God promised that He would spare the city for the sake of only ten righteous.

God intervening in our world is not dependent on the wickedness of the wicked but on the righteousness of the righteous.

 **takeaway**

In what areas are you engaged with interceding for the world around you—are you one of the righteous for whom God will spare the city?

reflect

_____

_____

_____

_____

_____

_____

_____

_____

_____

_____

⏰ minute 99

WORTH IT

By God's grace, I have been blessed to build several churches in my lifetime. One of the biggest challenges in a construction project is trying to fit the church's growing needs into an attainable budget. Purchase the land, design the project, develop the land, and with what is left, build the building. Often, a church has to cut corners and sacrifice needs to accommodate the bottom line of the financial plan.

JESUS HAS PROVIDED FOR OUR EVERY NEED, AND STILL HAS RICHES TO SPARE.

The Bible states that we are "God's building." In Luke 14:28, Jesus adds, "Suppose one of you wants to build a tower. Won't you first sit down and estimate the cost to see if you have enough money to complete it?"

Don't you think God takes His own advice? Before you were born, God considered exactly what it would cost to build you into the person He wanted you to be. He counted the astronomical cost, spread his arms out wide on a splintered cross, and said, "You are worth it." Without cutting out a space or shrinking His plan, Jesus has provided for our every need, and still has riches to spare.

Oh, how unsearchable, inexhaustible, and thoroughly exceptional is God's plan for each of us.

 **takeaway**

What comes to your mind when you think of God's "unsearchable, inexhaustible, exceptional" plan for you?

reflect

_____

_____

_____

_____

_____

_____

_____

_____

_____

_____

GROW GRASS

People who have been in church a long time are often taken back by my very uncomplicated philosophy of ministry. Sunday visitors often hand me their resumes and books, looking to obtain a quick platform for their business or ministry. But I have pastored long enough to understand that before I get impressed by your title, I need to see you wearing a towel.

John 13:4 says Jesus got up from the last supper, took off his outer clothing, and wrapped a towel around his waist and began to wash his disciples' feet. To truly lead, one must first learn to serve.

BEFORE I GET IMPRESSED BY YOUR TITLE, I NEED TO SEE YOU WEARING A TOWEL.

As a servant leader, my ambition is not so much to build a ministry but to build and serve people. When people are strong, the organization is strong. The focus is never on getting more sheep but on growing healthy grass, maintaining a safe environment, and keeping an open door. When church leaders have healthy attitudes, the result will be a healthy and growing congregation.

 **takeaway**

What are some ways you express servant leadership in your life, work, family, etc.?

reflect

_____

_____

_____

_____

_____

_____

_____

_____

_____

_____

_____

⏱ minute 101

ORGANIZED RELIGION

I often hear people say, "I am against organized religion." I often want to ask, "Are you saying you are for disorganized religion? Are you for chaos? Organization is a fundamental principle of success."

Ecclesiastes 4:9–10 says two are better than one, because they have a good return for their work. Certain outcomes can only be arrived at through cooperation. This is why darkness tries so desperately to keep us apart.

IF YOU CAN ALWAYS WALK ALONE, IT IS PROBABLY BECAUSE YOU ARE NOT GOING VERY FAR.

Ecclesiastes continues. "If one falls down, his friend can help him up." We need each other. Then it says, "But pity the man who falls and has no one to help him up." Certain help will not be available in our lives unless we have strong relationships.

It is vital that each of us discovers the power of maintaining healthy connections with other people. If you can always walk alone, it is probably because you are not going very far.

takeaway

If you tend to be a loner, what are some ways in which you can invite others into your life so you don't walk alone?

reflect

_____

_____

_____

_____

_____

_____

_____

_____

_____

_____

⏱ minute 102

MOVING

I have tarried with many people during the last moments of their lives. However, one lady I will never forget. She said she was not welcome in other churches and came to our services as a last resort. She eventually responded to the message of salvation and was marvelously born again.

It was in the late '90s or early 2000s, and she was suffering from AIDS. But she was so hungry for the Sunday teaching that she would inject her feet with needles to numb the pain so that she could come to church. Eventually, her disease ran its course, and she was moved into a hospice center.

She did not want to go, but she eventually went there to spend her final days. A few days later, she looked at me with such joy shining in her face that it scared me. She said, "Pastor, I want to go home." I thought she meant back to her apartment. I told her that she could not. She looked at me, reprimanding me with her eyes, as if I of all people should have understood what she meant.

Second Corinthians 5:8 (ESV) declares to be away from the body is to be at home with the Lord. She was no longer resistant, and she was ready to move one last time.

 **takeaway**

Although you may be young and healthy, in what ways to cultivate an awareness of the shortness of life?

reflect

_____

_____

_____

_____

_____

_____

_____

_____

_____

_____

_____

⏱ minute 103

HOW COULD A LOVING GOD SEND PEOPLE TO HELL?

People often ask with incredulity, "How could a loving God send people to hell?" I think the more appropriate question is this: "How could anyone be so evil that they would reject the mercy of a loving God who would spare them?" Jesus said in Matthew 25:41, "The king will say to those on his left, 'Depart from me, you who are cursed, into the eternal fire prepared for the devil and his angels.'"

We need to consider two things about hell: First, it was not prepared for people but the Devil. Those of us who go to hell are uninvited guests. We force ourselves in by pushing past God's grace and mercy and insisting on the consequences.

Secondly, if all people do, day and night, in heaven is celebrate God's goodness, and you can't stand twenty minutes of worship in church, how are you going to handle an eternity of praise? Unless your heart is changed, heaven would be like hell to you. God does not arbitrarily send people to hell. We send ourselves by our unwillingness to embrace His mercy and love.

 **takeaway**

How does an awareness of the reality of heaven and hell influence the way you live your life?

 **reflect**

_____

_____

_____

_____

_____

_____

_____

_____

_____

_____

_____

_____

⏰ minute 104

LOYALTY

In Job 2:2–4, the Lord said to Satan, "Have you considered my servant Job?" ... "Skin for skin!" Satan replied. "A man will give all he has for his own life ... Strike his flesh and bones, and he will surely curse you to your face."

Satan is a cynic. He was implying that Job obeyed God only because of what God *did* for him, not because of what God *meant* to him. Trials don't come because God does not care for us but because the Devil is cynical about our faith.

When I was in my late 20's and early 30's, doctors could not cure me of a chronic disease. I was in debt, my board was talking of firing me, and friends and family were few and far between. It seemed like everything I touched fell apart. I put on a front during the day, but when my wife and kids were asleep, I would go into my closet, kneel on the floor, and worship with tears.

I did not understand all that was happening in my life, but I could not abandon the One who would never abandon me. I would say with Job, "Though he slay me, yet will I trust in him." (Job 13:15, NKJV) Sometimes faith is spelled l–o–y–a–l–t–y.

 **takeaway**

When was a time when your suffering was so great that you were tempted to abandon God?

reflect

_____

_____

_____

_____

_____

_____

_____

_____

_____

_____

_____

⏱ minute 105

JESUS LOVES ME

Paul says in Romans 8:38–39,

> For I am convinced that neither death nor life, neither angels nor demons, neither the present nor the future, nor any powers, neither height nor depth, nor anything else in all creation, will be able to separate us from the love of God that is in Christ Jesus our Lord.

PAUL CHANGED THE WORLD BECAUSE HE WAS CONVINCED OF ONE THING: THAT GOD LOVED HIM.

What does God want us to be convinced of? Convinced that we are always right? That certain things will go as planned? No. Paul changed the world because he was convinced of one thing: that God loved him. Are you fully persuaded, certain, and knowing beyond a shadow of a doubt that sickness or health, life or death, the angelic or demonic, time or space, or thinkable or unthinkable cannot get between you and God's love for you? Our theology has become too complicated when we forget the simple lyrics we learned as children. "Jesus loves me, this I know, for the Bible tells me so." Jesus said, "Truly, I say to you, whoever does not receive the kingdom of God like a child shall not enter it." (Luke 18:17, ESV)

 **takeaway**

Are you convinced that God loves you? How does this reality change the way you look at life?

reflect

_____

_____

_____

_____

_____

_____

_____

_____

_____

_____

_____

⏱ minute 106

THE LOTTERY

A mathematician made an observation that stuck with me. "God is so big that all of eternity fits on his insides." We tend to see the past, present, and future in a linear fashion, but God stands outside of time and looks at the past, present, and future all at once.

MATHEMATICALLY SPEAKING, IT IS OVER ONE MILLION TIMES MORE LIKELY TO WIN THE LOTTERY THAN FOR JESUS NOT TO BE THE MESSIAH.

In Isaiah 46:9–10 (NKJV), God says, "I am God, and there is no other... I make known the end from the beginning, from ancient times, what is still to come..." Years ago, two scientists calculated the probability that just eight predictions of the Messiah would be fulfilled in one person: place of birth, type of death, gender, mother, ethnicity, etc. He came up with odds of one in one hundred quadrillion. Astronomical! Mathematically speaking, it is over one million times more likely to win the lottery than for Jesus not to be the Messiah. You are facing far better odds investing your dollar in God's kingdom this Sunday than buying your next lottery ticket.

takeaway

How does the greatness of God affect your view of Him and the world He made?

reflect

_____

_____

_____

_____

_____

_____

_____

_____

_____

_____

_____

⏱ minute 107

MAKING TIME TO PRAY

For the last 20 years, I have served a church with a lot of needs. I have led four services each Sunday with meetings in-between. I teach another three to five times a week, conduct funerals, weddings, and hospital visitations, serve families in crisis, counsel, address media, oversee our administrative and organizational needs, and the list goes on. Spoiler alert! I don't get more hours in a day because I am called to the ministry. I get 24 hours like everybody else.

THE TRUTH IS YOU DON'T HAVE ENOUGH TIME NOT TO PRAY.

Charles Spurgeon once said, "I have so much to do today that I shall never get through it with less than three hours' prayer."[20] I am learning the more I have to do, the more I need to make time for God. For every hour I invest in prayer, I am saved double by not having to do the extra work of fixing things I would otherwise break.

You think you don't have time to pray, but the truth is you don't have enough time not to pray.

 **takeaway**

How have you addressed the challenge of making time to pray?

reflect

_____

_____

_____

_____

_____

_____

_____

_____

_____

_____

_____

_____

_____

minute 108

PUNISHED FOR OUR PEACE

Would you worship a loving God even though He was unjust? You might try to appease Him but could never truly respect such a God. There is only one place in history where God's absolute love and justice collide. Isaiah 53:5 says of Jesus, "But he was pierced for our transgressions, he was crushed for our iniquities; the punishment that brought us peace was on him."

THE CROSS WAS GOD REACHING INTO HIS OWN POCKET TO PAY THE PENALTY FOR OUR SINS.

Justice required that sin be punished, but mercy desired to spare the guilty. This reminds me of a story about a judge in a small town. His son was caught speeding and had to appear before his father in court. It was a test, but the father had to find his son guilty. After the hearing, he took off his black robe and reached into his own pocket and paid his son's fine.

The cross was God reaching into His own pocket to pay the penalty for our sins. The punishment that brought us peace was paid by Him. What happened on Calvary was the most profound example of integrity, wisdom, and mercy ever found in one place.

takeaway

As you consider the price Jesus paid for your sin, what is your response?

reflect

_____

_____

_____

_____

_____

_____

_____

_____

_____

_____

_____

_____

⏱ minute 109

WOUNDED SO WE COULD BE HEALED

Few people question whether God forgives, but many debate whether Jesus still heals. In the first century, the debate was reversed. People believed that God healed but questioned whether Jesus had the authority to forgive.

In Luke 5:20–24, some men brought a sick man to Jesus who stated, "Your sins are forgiven." The Pharisees began thinking, "Who is this fellow who speaks blasphemy? Who can forgive sins but God alone?"

Listen to Christ's reply: "Which is *easier* to say, 'Your sins are forgiven,' or to say, 'Get up and walk?' But I want you to know that the Son of Man has authority on earth to forgive sins." So he said to the paralyzed man, "I tell you, get up, take your mat, and go home."

Jesus used a visible healing to confirm invisible forgiveness.

First Peter 2:24 says, "By his wounds we have been healed." According to Peter, the cross not only provides forgiveness but also healing. Have you embraced an "easier to say" tradition or a "harder to do" truth?

 **takeaway**

What does Jesus' ability to forgive
your sins say about His ability to
meet other needs you may have?

reflect

_____

_____

_____

_____

_____

_____

_____

_____

_____

_____

_____

⏰ minute 110

CURSED SO WE COULD BE BLESSED

What is the significance of the cross? Let's look at another blessing Jesus made available through Calvary. Galatians 3:13 says, "Christ redeemed us from the curse of the law by becoming a curse for us."

Some do not want to admit that curses exist because the idea sounds so primitive. But if they do not exist, why would Scripture inform us that Jesus died to redeem us from them? Sin is not only evil, but it is also cursed.

When we sin, we open our lives to sin's effects. Sin carries, in itself, the seeds of punishment and destruction. God does not randomly curse us, but our sins will. How do we break curses in our lives? Recognize the destructive patterns in our lives, turn to God, and renounce every belief and behavior that has opened the door to Satan. Proverbs 26:2 says an undeserved curse will not rest. A curse cannot rest on you if you learn to rest in the redeeming work of Jesus, on Calvary's cross.

 **takeaway**

Are there destructive patterns in your life that have opened the door to Satan that you should renounce?

💬 **reflect**

_____

_____

_____

_____

_____

_____

_____

_____

_____

_____

_____

_____

REJECTED SO WE COULD BE ACCEPTED

Before Jesus spoke His last time from the cross, He said, "It is finished." But what was finished? Mathew 27:46 reports that moments earlier, "About three in the afternoon, Jesus cried in a loud voice... 'My God, my God why have you forsaken me?'" Jesus was rejected, so we could be accepted.

Five verses later, the Bible records, "The curtain of the temple was torn from top to bottom." Josephus, an ancient historian, reported that the veil was four inches thick, was changed every year, and that horses tied to each side could not pull it apart. For thousands of years, God's presence resided primarily in a little room called the Most Holy Place that was shielded by this curtain. Only the high priest entered this room; this happened only once a year, while he was carrying atonement blood.

The veil was torn from the top, because God was indicating that the way into to His presence was not opened by the works of a mere man but by the work of heaven's Son. God never wanted to live in a little room but desires to live in the hearts of His people. The curtain has been torn, but it is up to us to choose to cross this threshold into His presence.

 **takeaway**

How are you pursuing the relationship with God that was made accessible to you through Jesus' work on the cross?

reflect

_____

_____

_____

_____

_____

_____

_____

_____

_____

_____

section 15
LEADERSHIP

⏱ minute 112

LEADERSHIP MYTH #1

There was a time when twice a year, I would travel to Ethiopia to train leaders for John Maxwell's EQUIP. I want to share one of the seven deadliest leadership myths that I taught in my sessions with the Ethiopian leaders.

Myth #1 is the idea that a person cannot lead unless he or she is on the top.[21] This is the misconception that leadership comes from simply having a position or title. Nothing could be farther from the truth!

In Exodus 18, we discover that Moses needed some guidance. It is surprising that God did not use a titled leader from within Israel to help Moses but his father-in-law, Jethro. Exodus 18:24 says, "Moses listened to his father-in-law and did everything he said." No matter your title, if people respect you, you can positively influence them.

The true measure of leadership is influence—nothing more, nothing less. A person who has respect can influence others from any position.

 **takeaway**

How have you observed the difference between leadership "position" and leadership "influence"?

reflect

_____

_____

_____

_____

_____

_____

_____

_____

_____

_____

LEADERSHIP MYTH #2

The second most dangerous leadership myth is this notion: "When I get to the top, then I'll learn to lead."[22] Climbing into the cockpit of a jet airplane does not make you a pilot any more than having people call you "Pastor" will make you a good pastor. Becoming a good leader is a lifelong process. There is nothing automatic about it. Good leadership is learned in the trenches.

If you do not develop your leadership skills when the stakes are small and the risks are low, you are likely to get into major trouble if you have to learn after you are placed in high-level leadership. When the opportunity to lead comes, it is too late to prepare!

I want you to think about who God selected to replace Moses after his death. It was Joshua, the man the Bible calls "Moses' aid." Joshua served approximately forty years under the leadership of Moses before God released him into his own. It took forty years of training before Joshua was ready to lead. So be careful about trying to lead before you are ready.

 **takeaway**

Can you recall a time when you or someone you know was placed in a position of leadership prematurely?

reflect

_____

_____

_____

_____

_____

_____

_____

_____

_____

_____

_____

⏰ minute 114

LEADERSHIP MYTH #3

The third myth we want to look at is what John Maxwell calls, "The Influence Myth." He said, "If I were at the top, then people would follow me."[23] Someone may give you a leadership title or position, but this will not make you a genuine leader. A position does not make a leader; the leader makes the position.

In Second Chronicles 10:6–19, Solomon's son Rehoboam became king, but it almost immediately fell apart. He decided to ignore the advice of his father's long-time counselors and listened to the advice of Pookie and Ray-Ray because they were his childhood friends. Just because you have known someone a long time, does not mean the person knows what he or she is talking about.

As a result of Rehoboam's foolish approach, the nation was irreparably split. Ten tribes revolted, and only Judah and Benjamin remained under his authority. It is far easier to lead in your imagination than in real life. An organization will always grow or shrink to match the competence level of the person in charge.

 **takeaway**

What are areas of competence that you can cultivate to prepare for a future leadership opportunity?

reflect

_____

_____

_____

_____

_____

_____

_____

_____

_____

_____

_____

⏰ minute 115

LEADERSHIP MYTH #4

Have you ever said to yourself, "If I were in charge, things sure would be different around here?" Listen to what King David's son, Absalom, said in Second Samuel 15:4 to anyone who would listen. "If only I were appointed judge in the land! Then everyone who has a complaint or case could come to me and I would see that they receive justice." The idea was that if he was on top, he would be more in control.[24]

There is nothing wrong in having a desire to improve your organization. But those without experience in leading will almost certainly overestimate the amount of control the person has at the top. The higher you go, the more you discover that many factors control an organization. Your position never gives you total control.

The Bible says that Absalom eventually seized the kingdom from his father but things quickly fell apart. It can sometimes be easier to criticize something than to improve it.

takeaway

Recall a time when you criticized someone in authority, only to discover later that you would have made the same decisions they did.

reflect

_____

_____

_____

_____

_____

_____

_____

_____

_____

_____

⏲ minute 116

LEADERSHIP MYTH #5

Today, we are going to look at the fifth myth people entertain. "When I get to the top, I'll no longer be limited."[25] Many people think that leadership is a ticket to freedom. Have you had thoughts like these from time to time?

- "When I get to the top, I'll have it made."

- "When I finally climb the organizational ladder, I'll have time to rest."

- "When I control the organization, I'll be able to do whatever I want."

These ideas are pure fantasy. On the contrary, when you move up in an organization, the weight of responsibility only increases. Usually, the more you move up the ladder in an organization, the responsibility you take on increases much faster than the amount of authority you receive. The higher you go, the more is expected of you and there is less room for error.

Jesus summed it up best by saying, "If anyone would be first, he must be servant of all." (Mark 9:35, ESV) The higher up you go, the more service is required and the less freedom you have.

 **takeaway**

What leadership "fantasies" did you believe before you were given a position of leadership?

reflect

_____

_____

_____

_____

_____

_____

_____

_____

_____

_____

_____

⏱ minute 117

LEADERSHIP MYTH #6

The sixth deadliest leadership myth is this: "I can't reach my potential if I'm not the top leader."[26] People should strive for the top of their effectiveness, not to be at the top of the organization. Each of us should work to reach our potential but not necessarily the CEO's chair.

Sometimes, you can make the greatest impact from somewhere other than the first seat. Joseph was such an example. He was sold into slavery to an Egyptian official. In spite of his low position, his faithful leadership always resulted in promotion. Genesis 39:6 & 22 says, "Potiphar left everything he had in Joseph's care ... he did not concern himself with anything except the food he ate."

Next, Joseph was unfairly sent to prison. In spite of his incarceration, Scripture records that "the warden put Joseph in charge of all those held in the prison, and he was made responsible for all that was done there." All of this was preparation for his final #2 position when he became the senior aide to Pharaoh.

Joseph never held the top seat, but God used him to save his family and people on several continents from certain disaster. Joseph became one of the most relevant biblical leaders of his era not because he was in the top seat but because he served well in the #2 chair.

takeaway

What experiences have you had leading from the "#2 chair" and what have you learned from them?

reflect

_____

_____

_____

_____

_____

_____

_____

_____

_____

_____

_____

⏱ minute 118

LEADERSHIP MYTH #7

We are going to look at the final leadership myth: The All-or-Nothing Myth. "If I can't get to the top, then I won't try to lead at all."[27] It is the mentality that says since I am not calling all the shots on the playground, I am going to take all my toys and go home.

Some people define success as being "on top." So, if they do not get the position they want, they become bitter, cynical, and often a hindrance to those who are in top levels of leadership. Paul says in Second Corinthians 10:13, "We will not boast beyond proper limits, but will confine our boasting to the sphere of service God himself has assigned to us." In other words, Paul found out what God had assigned him to do and became content with staying in his own lane.

A mentor once told a proud mentee, "You may think that you are the sharpest knife in the drawer, but you are not. You should learn to celebrate the fact that you are in the drawer at all." We must focus on fulfilling our own potential, versus competing with someone else's.

takeaway

If you don't get your way, what is your instinctive response—and how do you mitigate it?

reflect

_____

_____

_____

_____

_____

_____

_____

_____

_____

_____

_____

⏰ minute 119

BOB

This one EQUIP lesson leapt off the page for me, and I want to enlarge upon it and share it with you. The heading was this: "When Bob Has a Problem with Everyone, Bob Is Usually the Problem."[28]

How Do You Recognize a "Bob"?

1. Bob is a problem *carrier*. Like a contagious disease, people like Bob carry a "virus" that magnetically attracts negative situations.

2. Bob is a problem *finder*. It takes talent to fix problems, not to find them. Bob has eyes to see problems everywhere.

3. Bob is a problem *creator*. Bob seems to generate problems wherever he goes.

4. Bob is a problem *receiver*. Other people seem to know that Bob is a safe place to gossip, complain, and insult others. Remember that flies are attracted to stink.

My apologies to everyone named Bob, but begin to spot the Bobs in your life or organization, and make sure that Bob isn't you.

 **takeaway**

Which "Bob" do you most struggle
with being?

reflect

_____

_____

_____

_____

_____

_____

_____

_____

_____

_____

_____

_____

LEADERSHIP PYRAMID

An essential part of being a good leader is knowing which rights to give up and which ones to fight for. In First Corinthians 9:3–5 & 12, Paul says, "This is my defense to those who sit on judgment on me." If you are going to be a leader, you have to get used to people judging you. He continues. "Don't we who are on missionary assignments for God have a right to decent accommodations, and a right to receive support for us and our families? (MSG) But we did not use these rights. Instead we put up with anything rather than hinder the gospel of Christ." Paul rightfully received compensation from other churches, but he knew that if he received it from this church, it would have created a scandal.

THE GREATER OUR CALLING, THE MORE RIGHTS WE WILL AT TIMES NEED TO FORFEIT.

The greater our calling, the more rights we will at times need to forfeit. Ministry is never a pyramid with its leaders on the top. True leaders see themselves at the bottom holding others up. Find a solid church and get on the bottom, so you can be on top!

takeaway

What rights have you forfeited as a leader, and how has it allowed you to develop yourself and others more effectively?

reflect

_____

_____

_____

_____

_____

_____

_____

_____

_____

_____

ABOUT THE AUTHOR

Dr. Derek Grier currently serves as the founding pastor of Grace Church in Dumfries, Virginia. Grace Church began in 1998 with 12 people and has grown to more than 5,000 members. His passion for serving people led him to establish over 50 life-changing ministries within Grace Church. His radio and television programs can be heard and viewed in over 2 billion homes across the globe, and more than 60 million homes in the United States.

Dr. Grier was ordained a bishop in 2008 by Dr. Myles Munroe. He currently mentors hundreds of Christian leaders and business owners through the Renaissance Leadership Network. Dr. Grier serves on several boards—including the board of directors for the Evangelical Council for Financial Accountability (ECFA), which provides accreditation to leading Christian nonprofit organizations that faithfully demonstrate standards for financial accountability and transparency. He has also served as an associate trainer for Equip, founded by John Maxwell.

Dr. Grier's uncompromising approach to preaching and teaching the gospel has helped him lead Grace Church in phenomenal growth. In 2013, *Outreach* magazine listed Grace Church as one of the fastest growing churches in the nation and among the top 100 fastest growing of all churches. In 2014, Grace was listed in *Outreach* magazine's annual "100 Fastest Growing Churches in America" as the 7th fastest growing church in the United States.

Dr. Grier studied business administration at Howard University and earned a Master of Education degree from Regent University. He holds a Doctorate in Practical Ministry from Wagner University. Dr. Grier received an honorary doctorate from Beulah Heights University, one of the oldest seminaries in the United States. He has received numerous awards and was honored in the United States Congressional Record on several occasions.

Dr. Grier is President of Virginia Bible College and is often asked to address elite military and governmental agencies. He has received multiple invitations to the White House and is regularly sought out by political leaders from both sides.

He is also the author of several books, including his latest release, *When God Stops,* to be released by T. Nelson Publishing in 2019.

Dr. Grier and his wife, Yeromitou, reside in northern Virginia and have two sons: Derek Jr. and David.

To Contact the Author

Follow Dr. Grier on social media.

Facebook: **www.Facebook.com/GraceChurchVA**

Twitter: **www.Twitter.com/GraceChurchVA**

YouTube: **www.Youtube.com/GraceChurchvaTV**

You can also stream live on Sundays and Wednesdays at **www.Lifestream.tv/gracechurch**.

For more information, visit our websites at **www.DerekGrier.com** or **www.GraceChurchVA.org**.

Next Steps

To continue your journey towards a more enriched, fulfilling and productive life with God, visit: www.ahigherplan.com.

NOTES

Section 1: Happiness

1. *Brainy Quote*, www.brainyquote.com/quotes/quotes/a/
abrahamlin100845.html (accessed January 7, 2009).

2. *Brainy Quote*, www.goodreads.com/author/
quotes/15151.Zora_Neale_Hurston (accessed January 7,
2009).

Section 2: Marriage and Family Relationships

3. *Think Exist.com*, http://thinkexist.com/quotation/
people_do_not_care_how_much_you_know_until_
they/346868.html (accessed January 7, 2009).

Section 4: Process

4. Seneca quote available at http://thinkexist.com/
quotes/with/keyword/in_his_right_mind/ (accessed
January 8, 2009).

5. Michael Jordan quote available at http://www.
brainyquote.com/quotes/authors/m/michael_jordan.html
(accessed January 8, 2009).

6. Frederick Douglass quote available at http://
thinkexist.com/quotation/if_there_is_no_struggle-there_
is_no_progress/206199.html (accessed January 8, 2009).

Section 5: Preparation

7. Abraham Lincoln quote available at http://thinkexist.
com/quotation/if_i_had_eight_hours_to_chop_down_a_
tree-i-d/194268.html (accessed January 8, 2009).

Section 8: Wisdom

8. Helen Keller quote available at http://www. brainyquote.com/quotes/authors/h/helen_keller.html (accessed January 8, 2009).

9. Charles Stanley, *A Moment of Weakness*, www. intouch.org/magazine/content.aspx?topic=A-Moment-of-Weakness-Devotional#.UeaZ5l1QEwA (accessed July 1, 2013)

Section 9: Character

10. R. T. Kendall, *Controlling the Tongue* (Lake Mary, FL: Charisma House, 2007).

Section 11: Self-Esteem

11. Frederick Douglass quote available at We the People, http://www.givemeliberty.org/aboutus.htm (accessed January 21, 2009).

12. From Franklin D. Roosevelt's Inaugural Address, March 4, 1933, in *The Public Papers of Franklin D. Roosevelt, Volume Two: The Year of Crisis*, 1933, ed. Samuel Rosenman (New York: Random House, 1938).

13. Dr. Myles Munroe, from his address at the International Third World Leaders Association Conference, 2006.

Section 12: A Spirit of Excellence

14. Michael J. Fox quote available at http://www. brainyquote.com/quotes/authors/m/michael_j_fox.html (accessed January 9, 2009).

Section 13: Personal Growth

15. http://www.entheos.com/quotes/by_topic/Ralph +waldo+emerson.

16. http://lyricsfreak.com/k/knny+rogers/the+gambler.20077886.html.

17. *Equip* Volume 1, Notebook 6: "An In-Depth Journey into Transformational Leadership," Lesson 3: The Leader's Time: Tick, Tock, Manage the Clock. P. 14, 2004.

18. Maxwell, John. *Today Matters: 12 Daily Practices to Guarantee Tomorrow's Success.*

19. http://thinkexist.com/quotation/if-you-can-control-a-man-s-thinking-you-don-t/821594.html.

Section 14: Relationships

20. The Spurgeon Archive: "Pray without Ceasing," March 10, 1872. http:www.spurgeon.org/sermons/1039.htm.

Section 15: Leadership

21. *Volume 2, Notebook 3: "360 Degree Leader,"* Lesson 1: The Myths of Leading from the Middle of an Organization. P. 2, 2004.

22. *Volume 2 Notebook 3: "360 Degree Leader,"* Lesson 1: The Myths of Leading from the Middle of an Organization. P. 3, 2004.

23. *Volume 2, Notebook 3: "360 Degree Leader,"* Lesson 1: The Myths of Leading from the Middle of an Organization. P. 3. 2004.

24. *Volume 2, Notebook 3: "360 Degree Leader,"* Lesson 1: The Myths of Leading from the Middle of an Organization. P. 4, 2004.

25. *Volume 2, Notebook 3: "360 Degree Leader,"* Lesson 1: The Myths of Leading from the Middle of an Organization. P. 5, 2004.

26. *Volume 2, Notebook 3: "360 Degree Leader,"* Lesson 1: The Myths of Leading from the Middle of an Organization. P. 6, 2004.

27. *Volume 2, Notebook 3: "360 Degree Leader,"* Lesson 1: The Myths of Leading from the Middle of an Organization. P. 6, 2004.

28. *Volume 2, Notebook 2: "Winning with People,"* Lesson 4: Can We Build Mutual Trust? Pp. 18–19, 2004.

BREAK FREE FROM
LIFE'S LIMITATIONS!

The DGM Growth Lab will help you accelerate your growth by helping you remove the barriers keeping you from growing and walking in God's best. YOUR PATHWAY TO LIVING BIG IS GROWTH. Here is how we'll help you grow:

Resources

An ongoing, immersive experience that provides you with tools, training and resources to propel you forward into your purpose.

Training

Every month, you'll receive multi-part training courses on relevant topics, and every week, you'll receive brand new, full-length teaching sessions.

Assessment

The Growth Lab comes with an assessment tool that helps you identify where you're stuck, and points you to resources to help you break free.

GET 30 DAYS FREE ACCESS

dgmgrowthlab.com